THE KING'S THRESHOLD ON BAILE'S STRAND. DEIRDRE. SHADOWY WATERS; BEING THE SECOND VOLUME OF THE COLLECTED WORKS IN VERSE AND PROSE. IMPRINTED AT THE SHAKESPEARE HEAD PRESS STRADFORD-ON-AVON MCMVIII

Published @ 2017 Trieste Publishing Pty Ltd

ISBN 9780649551736

The King's threshold on Baile's strand. Deirdre. Shadowy waters; being the second volume of the collected works in verse and prose. Imprinted at the Shakespeare head press Stradford-on-avon MCMVIII by William Butler Yeats

Edited by Trieste Publishing Pty Ltd.
Cover @ 2017

www.triestepublishing.com

WILLIAM BUTLER YEATS

THE KING'S THRESHOLD ON BAILE'S STRAND. DEIRDRE. SHADOWY WATERS; BEING THE SECOND VOLUME OF THE COLLECTED WORKS IN VERSE AND PROSE. IMPRINTED AT THE SHAKESPEARE HEAD PRESS STRADFORD-ON-AVON MCMVIII

 Trieste

THE KING'S THRESHOLD. ON
BAILE'S STRAND. DEIRDRE.
SHADOWY WATERS ❧ BEING
THE SECOND VOLUME OF
THE COLLECTED WORKS IN
VERSE & PROSE OF WILLIAM
BUTLER YEATS ❧ IMPRINTED
AT THE SHAKESPEARE HEAD
PRESS STRATFORD-ON-AVON
MCMVIII

CONTENTS

The friends that have it I do wrong
When ever I remake a song,
Should know what issue is at stake :
It is myself that I remake.

THE KING'S THRESHOLD

TO FRANK FAY

BECAUSE OF HIS BEAUTIFUL SPEAKING IN
THE CHARACTER OF SEANCHAN

PERSONS IN THE PLAY

KING GUAIRE

SEANCHAN (*pronounced* SHANAHAN)

HIS PUPILS

THE MAYOR OF KINVARA

TWO CRIPPLES

BRIAN (*an old servant*)

THE LORD HIGH CHAMBERLAIN

A SOLDIER

A MONK

COURT LADIES

TWO PRINCESSES

FEDELM

THE KING'S THRESHOLD.

Steps before the Palace of KING GUAIRE *at Gort.*
A table in front of steps at one side, with food
on it, and a bench by table. SEANCHAN *lying*
on steps. PUPILS *before steps.* KING *on the*
upper step before a curtained door.

KING.

I WELCOME you that have the mastery
Of the two kinds of Music: the one kind
Being like a woman, the other like a man.
Both you that understand stringed instruments,
And how to mingle words and notes together
So artfully, that all the Art's but Speech
Delighted with its own music; and you that
      carry
The long twisted horn, and understand
The heady notes that, being without words,
Can hurry beyond Time and Fate and Change.

For the high angels that drive the horse of
    Time—
The golden one by day, by night the silver—
Are not more welcome to one that loves the
    world
For some fair woman's sake.
                     I have called you hither
To save the life of your great master, Seanchan,
For all day long it has flamed up or flickered
To the fast cooling hearth.

OLDEST PUPIL.

                  When did he sicken?
Is it a fever that is wasting him?

KING.

No fever or sickness.   He has chosen death:
Refusing to eat or drink, that he may bring
Disgrace upon me; for there is a custom,
An old and foolish custom, that if a man
Be wronged, or think that he is wronged, and
    starve
Upon another's threshold till he die,
The common people, for all time to come,
Will raise a heavy cry against that threshold,
Even though it be the King's.

OLDEST PUPIL.

           My head whirls round;
I do not know what I am to think or say.
I owe you all obedience, and yet
How can I give it, when the man I have loved
More than all others, thinks that he is wronged
So bitterly, that he will starve and die
Rather than bear it?   Is there any man
Will throw his life away for a light issue?

KING.

It is but fitting that you take his side
Until you understand how light an issue
Has put us by the ears.   Three days ago
I yielded to the outcry of my courtiers—
Bishops, Soldiers, and Makers of the Law—
Who long had thought it against their dignity
For a mere man of words to sit amongst them
At my own table. When the meal was spread,
I ordered Seanchan to a lower table;
And when he pleaded for the poets' right,
Established at the establishment of the world,
I said that I was King, and that all rights
Had their original fountain in some king,
And that it was the men who ruled the world,
And not the men who sang to it, who should
      sit

Where there was the most honour.   My
  courtiers—
Bishops, Soldiers, and Makers of the Law—
Shouted approval; and amid that noise
Seanchan went out, and from that hour to this,
Although there is good food and drink beside
  him,
Has eaten nothing.   .

OLDEST PUPIL.

   I can breathe again.
You have taken a great burden from my mind,
For that old custom's not worth dying for.

KING.

Persuade him to eat or drink.   Till yesterday
I thought that hunger and weakness had been
  enough;
But finding them too trifling and too light
To hold his mouth from biting at the grave,
I called you hither, and all my hope's in you,
And certain of his neighbours and good
  friends
That I have sent for.   While he is lying there
Perishing, my good name in the world
Is perishing also.   I cannot give way,
Because I am King.   Because if I gave way,

My Nobles would call me a weakling, and it
    may be
The very throne be shaken.

OLDEST PUPIL.

              I will persuade him.
Your words had been enough persuasion, King;
But being lost in sleep or reverie,
He cannot hear them.

KING.

             Make him eat or drink.
Nor is it all because of my good name
I'd have him do it, for he is a man
That might well hit the fancy of a king,
Banished out of his country, or a woman's,
Or any other's that can judge a man
For what he is. But I that sit a throne,
And take my measure from the needs of the
    State,
Call his wild thought that overruns the measure,
Making words more than deeds, and his proud
    will
That would unsettle all, most mischievous,
And he himself a most mischievous man.

    [*He turns to go, and then returns again.*
Promise a house with grass and tillage land,

An annual payment, jewels and silken ware,
Or anything but that old right of the poets.

[*He goes into palace.*

OLDEST PUPIL.

The King did wrong to abrogate our right;
But Seanchan, who talks of dying for it,
Talks foolishly.   Look at us, Seanchan;
Waken out of your dream and look at us,
Who have ridden under the moon and all the
        day,
Until the moon has all but come again,
That we might be beside you.

SEANCHAN.

[*Half turning round, leaning on his elbow, and
        speaking as if in a dream.*]
                        I was but now
In Almhuin, in a great high-raftered house,
With Finn and Osgar. Odours of roast flesh
Rose round me, and I saw the roasting-spits;
And then the dream was broken, and I saw
Grania dividing salmon by a stream.

OLDEST PUPIL.

Hunger has made you dream of roasting flesh;
And though I all but weep to think of it,

The hunger of the crane, that starves himself
At the full moon because he is afraid
Of his own shadow and the glittering water,
Seems to me little more fantastical
Than this of yours.

SEANCHAN.

Why, that's the very truth.
It is as though the moon changed everything—
Myself and all that I can hear and see;
For when the heavy body has grown weak,
There's nothing that can tether the wild mind
That, being moonstruck and fantastical,
Goes where it fancies.   I had even thought
I knew your voice and face, but now the words
Are so unlikely that I needs must ask
Who is it that bids me put my hunger by.

OLDEST PUPIL.

I am your oldest pupil, Seanchan;
The one that has been with you many years—
So many, that you said at Candlemas
That I had almost done with school, and knew
All but all that poets understand.

SEANCHAN.

My oldest pupil?   No, that cannot be,

For it is some one of the courtly crowds
That have been round about me from sunrise,
And I am tricked by dreams; but I'll refute
      them.
At Candlemas I bid that pupil tell me
Why poetry is honoured, wishing to know
If he had any weighty argument
For distant countries and strange, churlish kings.
What did he answer?

OLDEST PUPIL.

                    I said the poets hung
Images of the life that was in Eden
About the child-bed of the world, that it,
Looking upon those images, might bear
Triumphant children.   But why must I stand
      here,
Repeating an old lesson, while you starve?

SEANCHAN.

Tell on, for I begin to know the voice.
What evil thing will come upon the world
If the Arts perish?

OLDEST PUPIL.

            If the Arts should perish,
The world that lacked them would be like a
      woman,

That looking on the cloven lips of a hare,
Brings forth a hare-lipped child.

SEANCHAN.

                                    But that's not all:
For when I asked you how a man should guard
Those images, you had an answer also,
If you're the man that you have claimed to be,
Comparing them to venerable things
God gave to men before he gave them wheat.

OLDEST PUPIL.

I answered—and the word was half your own—
That he should guard them as the Men of Dea
Guard their four treasures, as the Grail King
        guards
His holy cup, or the pale, righteous horse
The jewel that is underneath his horn,
Pouring out life for it as one pours out
Sweet heady wine. . . . But now I under-
        stand;
You would refute me out of my own mouth;
And yet a place at table, near the King,
Is nothing of great moment, Seanchan.
How does so light a thing touch poetry?

    [SEANCHAN *is now sitting up.   He still looks*
        dreamily in front of him.

SEANCHAN.

At Candlemas you called this poetry
One of the fragile, mighty things of God,
That die at an insult.

OLDEST PUPIL.

[*To other* PUPILS.]

                Give me some true answer,
For on that day we spoke about the Court,
And said that all that was insulted there
The world insulted, for the Courtly life,
Being the first comely child of the world,
Is the world's model. How shall I answer him?
Can you not give me some true argument?
I will not tempt him with a lying one.

YOUNGEST PUPIL.

O, tell him that the lovers of his music
Have need of him.

SEANCHAN.

                But I am labouring
For some that shall be born in the nick o' time,
And find sweet nurture, that they may have
        voices,
Even in anger, like the strings of harps;

And how could they be born to majesty
If I had never made the golden cradle?

YOUNGEST PUPIL.

[*Throwing himself at* SEANCHAN'S *feet.*]

Why did you take me from my father's fields?
If you would leave me now, what shall I love?
Where shall I go?   What shall I set my hand to?
And why have you put music in my ears,
If you would send me to the clattering houses?
I will throw down the trumpet and the harp,
For how could I sing verses or make music
With none to praise me, and a broken heart?

SEANCHAN.

What was it that the poets promised you,
If it was not their sorrow?   Do not speak.
Have I not opened school on these bare steps,
And are not you the youngest of my scholars?
And I would have all know that when all falls
In ruin, poetry calls out in joy,
Being the scattering hand, the bursting pod,
The victim's joy among the holy flame,
God's laughter at the shattering of the world.
And now that joy laughs out, and weeps and
      burns
On these bare steps.

C

YOUNGEST PUPIL.

O master, do not die!

OLDEST PUPIL.

Trouble him with no useless argument.
Be silent!   There is nothing we can do
Except find out the King and kneel to him,
And beg our ancient right.
                                      For here are some
To say whatever we could say and more,
And fare as badly.   Come, boy, that is no use.

[*Raises* YOUNGEST PUPIL.

If it seem well that we beseech the King,
Lay down your harps and trumpets on the
    stones
In silence, and come with me silently.
Come with slow footfalls, and bow all your
    heads,
For a bowed head becomes a mourner best.

[*They lay harps and trumpets down one by one,
    and then go out very solemnly and slowly,
    following one another.   Enter* MAYOR, TWO
    CRIPPLES, *and* BRIAN, *an old servant.   The*
    MAYOR, *who has been heard, before he came
    upon the stage, muttering* 'Chief Poet,'
    'Ireland,' *etc., crosses in front of* SEANCHAN

to the other side of the steps. BRIAN *takes
food out of basket. The* CRIPPLES *are watching
the basket. The* MAYOR *has an Ogham stick
in his hand.*

MAYOR.

[*As he crosses.*]

'Chief Poet,' 'Ireland,' 'Townsman,' 'Grazing
    land,'
Those are the words I have to keep in mind—
'Chief Poet,' 'Ireland,' 'Townsman,' 'Grazing
    land.'
I have the words. They are all upon the
    Ogham.
'Chief Poet,' 'Ireland,' 'Townsman,' 'Grazing
    land.'
But what's their order?

[*He keeps muttering over his speech during
what follows.*

FIRST CRIPPLE.

       The King were rightly served
If Seanchan drove his good luck away.
What's there about a king, that's in the world
From birth to burial like another man,
That he should change old customs, that were
    in it
As long as ever the world has been a world?

SECOND CRIPPLE.

If I were king I would not meddle with him,
For there is something queer about a poet.
I knew of one that would be making rhyme
Under a thorn at crossing of three roads.
He was as ragged as ourselves, and yet
He was no sooner dead than every thorn tree
From Inchy to Kiltartan withered away.

FIRST CRIPPLE.

The King is but a fool!

MAYOR.

I am getting ready.

FIRST CRIPPLE.

A poet has power from beyond the world,
That he may set our thoughts upon old times,
And lucky queens and little holy fish
That rise up every seventh year——

MAYOR.

Hush! hush!

FIRST CRIPPLE.

To cure the crippled.

MAYOR.

I am half ready now.

BRIAN.

There's not a mischief I'd begrudge the King
If it were any other——

MAYOR.

Hush! I am ready.

BRIAN.

That died to get it. I have brought out the
    food,
And if my master will not eat of it,
I'll home and get provision for his wake,
For .that's no great way off. Well, have your
    say,
But don't be long about it.

MAYOR.

[*Goes close to* SEANCHAN.]
                Chief Poet of Ireland,
I am the Mayor of your own town Kinvara,
And I am come to tell you that the news
Of this great trouble with the King of Gort
Has plunged us in deep sorrow—part for you,

Our honoured townsman, part for our good
town.

[*Begins to hesitate; scratching his head.*

But what comes now? Something about the
King.

BRIAN.

Get on! get on! The food is all set out.

MAYOR.

Don't hurry me.

FIRST CRIPPLE.

Give us a taste of it.
He'll not begrudge it.

SECOND CRIPPLE.

Let them that have their limbs
Starve if they will. We have to keep in mind
The stomach God has left us.

MAYOR.

Hush! I have it!
The King was said to be most friendly to us,
And we have reason, as you'll recollect,

For thinking that he was about to give
Those grazing lands inland we so much need,
Being pinched between the water and the
    stones.
Our mowers mow with knives between the
    stones;
The sea washes the meadows. You know well
We have asked nothing but what's reasonable.

SEANCHAN.

Reason in plenty. Yellowy white hair,
A hollow face, and not too many teeth.
How comes it he has been so long in the world
And not found Reason out?

    [*While saying this he has turned half round.
    He hardly looks at the* MAYOR.

BRIAN.

    [*Trying to pull* MAYOR *away.*]

                What good is there
In telling him what he has heard all day!
I will set food before him.

MAYOR.

    [*Shoving* BRIAN *away.*]

                Don't hurry me!

It's small respect you're showing to the town!
Get farther off! [*To* SEANCHAN.] We would
    not have you think,
Weighty as these considerations are,
That they have been as weighty in our minds
As our desire that one we take much pride in,
A man that's been an honour to our town,
Should live and prosper; therefore we beseech
    you
To give way in a matter of no moment,
A matter of mere sentiment—a trifle—
That we may always keep our pride in you.

> [*He finishes this speech with a pompous air,
> motions to* BRIAN *to bring the food to*
> SEANCHAN, *and sits on seat.*

BRIAN.

Master, master, eat this! It's not king's food,
That's cooked for everybody and nobody.
Here's barley-bread out of your father's oven,
And dulse from Duras.   Here is the dulse,
    your honour;
It's wholesome, and has the good taste of the sea.

> [*Takes dulse in one hand and bread in other
> and presses them into* SEANCHAN's *hands.*
> SEANCHAN *shows by his movement his
> different feeling to* BRIAN.

FIRST CRIPPLE.

He has taken it, and there'll be nothing left!

SECOND CRIPPLE.

Nothing at all; he wanted his own sort.
What's honey to a cat, corn to a dog,
Or a green apple to a ghost in a churchyard?

SEANCHAN.

[*Pressing food back into* BRIAN's *hands.*]
Eat it yourself, for you have come a journey,
And it may be eat nothing on the way.

BRIAN.

How could I eat it, and your honour starving!
It is your father sends it, and he cried
Because the stiffness that is in his bones
Prevented him from coming, and bid me tell
       you
That he is old, that he has need of you,
And that the people will be pointing at him,
And he not able to lift up his head,
If you should turn the King's favour away;
And he adds to it, that he cared you well,
And you in your young age, and that it's right
That you should care him now.

SEANCHAN.

[*Who is now interested.*]

And is that all?
What did my mother say?   /

BRIAN.

She gave no message;
For when they told her you had it in mind to
    starve,
Or get again the ancient right of the poets,
She said: 'No message can do any good.
He will not send the answer that you want.
We cannot change him.'   And she went
    indoors,
Lay down upon the bed, and turned her face
Out of the light.   And thereupon your father
Said: 'Tell him that his mother sends no
    message,
Albeit broken down and miserable.' [*A pause.*
Here's a pigeon's egg from Duras, and these
    others
Were laid by your own hens.

SEANCHAN.

She has sent no message.
Our mothers know us; they know us to the
    bone.

They knew us before birth, and that is why
They know us even better than the sweethearts
Upon whose breasts we have lain.
                              Go quickly ! Go
And tell them that my mother was in the right.
There is no answer. Go and tell them that.
Go tell them that she knew me.

MAYOR.

                              What is he saying ?
I never understood a poet's talk
More than the baa of a sheep !

> [*Comes over from seat.* SEANCHAN *turns away.*

                              You have not heard,
It may be, having been so much away,
How many of the cattle died last winter
From lacking grass, and that there was much
      sickness
Because the poor have nothing but salt fish
To live on through the winter ?

BRIAN.

                              Get away,
And leave the place to me ! It's my turn now,
For your sack's empty !

MAYOR.

Is it 'get away'!
Is that the way I'm to be spoken to!
Am I not Mayor?   Amn't I authority?
Amn't I in the King's place? Answer me that!

BRIAN.

Then show the people what a king is like:
Pull down old merings and root custom up,
Whitewash the dunghills, fatten hogs and
        geese,
Hang your gold chain about an ass's neck,
And burn the blessed thorn trees out of the
        fields,
And drive what's comely away!

MAYOR.

Holy Saint Coleman!

FIRST CRIPPLE.

Fine talk! fine talk! What else does the King
    do?
He fattens hogs and drives the poet away!

SECOND CRIPPLE.

He starves the song-maker!

FIRST CRIPPLE.

> He fattens geese!

MAYOR.

How dare you take his name into your mouth!
How dare you lift your voice against the King!
What would we be without him?

BRIAN.

> Why do you praise him?
I will have nobody speak well of him,
Or any other king that robs my master.

MAYOR.

And had he not the right to? and the right
To strike your master's head off, being the
      King,
Or yours or mine? I say, 'Long live the King!
Because he does not take our heads from us.'
Call out, 'Long life to him!'

BRIAN.

> Call out for him!
> *[Speaking at same time with* MAYOR.
There's nobody'll call out for him,
But smiths will turn their anvils,

The millers turn their wheels,
The farmers turn their churns,
The witches turn their thumbs,
'Till he be broken and splintered into pieces.

MAYOR.

[*At same time with* BRIAN.]

He might, if he'd a mind to it,
Be digging out our tongues,
Or dragging out our hair,
Or bleaching us like calves,
Or weaning us like lambs,
But for the kindness and the softness that is in
    him.

[*They gasp for breath.*

FIRST CRIPPLE.

I'll curse him till I drop !

[*Speaking at same time as* SECOND CRIPPLE
    and MAYOR *and* BRIAN, *who have begun
    again.*

The curse of the poor be upon him,
The curse of the widows upon him,
The curse of the children upon him,
The curse of the bishops upon him,
Until he be as rotten as an old mushroom !

SECOND CRIPPLE.

[*Speaking at same time as* FIRST CRIPPLE *and* MAYOR *and* BRIAN.

The curse of wrinkles be upon him!
Wrinkles where his eyes are,
Wrinkles where his nose is,
Wrinkles where his mouth is,
And a little old devil looking out of every
  wrinkle!

BRIAN.

[*Speaking at same time with* MAYOR *and* CRIPPLES.]
And nobody will sing for him,
And nobody will hunt for him,
And nobody will fish for him,
And nobody will pray for him,
But ever and always curse him and abuse him.

MAYOR.

[*Speaking at same time with* CRIPPLES *and* BRIAN.]
What good is in a poet?
Has he money in a stocking,
Or cider in the cellar,
Or flitches in the chimney,
Or anything anywhere but his own idleness?

[BRIAN *seizes* MAYOR.

MAYOR.

Help! help!   Am I not in authority?

BRIAN.

That's how I'll shout for the King!

MAYOR.

Help! help!   Am I not in the King's place?

BRIAN.

I'll teach him to be kind to the poor!

MAYOR.

Help! help!   Wait till we are in Kinvara!

FIRST CRIPPLE.
[*Beating* MAYOR *on the legs with crutch.*]
I'll shake the royalty out of his legs!

SECOND CRIPPLE.
[*Burying his nails in* MAYOR's *face.*]
I'll scrumble the ermine out of his skin!
    [*The* CHAMBERLAIN *comes down steps shout-*
    ing, 'Silence! silence! silence!'

CHAMBERLAIN.

How dare you make this uproar at the doors,
Deafening the very greatest in the land,
As if the farmyards and the rookeries
Had all been emptied!

FIRST CRIPPLE.

It is the Chamberlain.

[CRIPPLES *go out.*

CHAMBERLAIN.

Pick up the litter there, and get you gone!
Be quick about it!   Have you no respect
For this worn stair, this all but sacred door,
Where suppliants and tributary kings
Have passed, and the world's glory knelt in silence?
Have you no reverence for what all other men
Hold honourable?

BRIAN.

If I might speak my mind,
I'd say the King would have his luck again
If he would let my master have his rights.

CHAMBERLAIN.

Pick up your litter!   Take your noise away!
Make haste, and get the clapper from the bell!

D

BRIAN.

[Putting last of food into basket.]
What do the great and powerful care for rights
That have no armies!

> [CHAMBERLAIN *begins shoving them out with
> his staff.*

MAYOR.

My lord, I am not to blame.
I'm the King's man, and they attacked me for it.

BRIAN.

We have our prayers, our curses and our prayers,
And we can give a great name or a bad one.

> [MAYOR *is shoving* BRIAN *out before him with
> one hand. He keeps his face to* CHAMBER-
> LAIN, *and keeps bowing. The* CHAMBERLAIN
> *shoves him with his staff.*

MAYOR.

We could not make the poet eat, my lord.

> [CHAMBERLAIN *shoves him with staff.*

Much honoured [*is shoved again*]—honoured to
    speak with you, my lord;
But I'll go find the girl that he's to marry.
She's coming, but I'll hurry her, my lord.

Between ourselves, my lord [*is shoved again*],
    she is a great coaxer.
Much honoured, my lord.   O, she's the girl
    to do it;
For when the intellect is out, my lord,
Nobody but a woman's any good.
                        [*Is shoved again.*
Much honoured, my lord [*is shoved again*],
    much honoured, much honoured!

  [*Is shoved out, shoving* BRIAN *out before him.*

  [*All through this scene, from the outset of the
    quarrel,* SEANCHAN *has kept his face turned
    away, or hidden in his cloak.   While the*
    CHAMBERLAIN *has been speaking, the* SOLDIER
    and the MONK *have come out of the palace.
    The* MONK *stands on top of steps at one side,
    *SOLDIER *a little down steps at the other side.*
    COURT LADIES *are seen at opening in the palace
    curtain behind* SOLDIER.   CHAMBERLAIN *is in
    the centre.*

CHAMBERLAIN.

[*To* SEANCHAN.]

Well, you must be contented, for your work
Has roused the common sort against the King,
And stolen his authority.   The State
Is like some orderly and reverend house,

Wherein the master, being dead of a sudden,
The servants quarrel where they have a mind to,
And pilfer here and there.

   [*Pause, finding that* SEANCHAN *does not answer.*
                        How many days
Will you keep up this quarrel with the King,
And the King's nobles, and myself, and all,
Who'd gladly be your friends, if you would let
   them?

                  [*Going near to* MONK.

If you would try, you might persuade him,
   father.
I cannot make him answer me, and yet
If fitting hands would offer him the food,
He might accept it.

            MONK.

            Certainly I will not.
I've made too many homilies, wherein
The wanton imagination of the poets
Has been condemned, to be his flatterer.
If pride and disobedience are unpunished
Who will obey?

            CHAMBERLAIN.
   [*Going to other side towards* SOLDIER.]
               If you would speak to him,

You might not find persuasion difficult,
With all the devils of hunger helping you.

SOLDIER.

I will not interfere, and if he starve
For being obstinate and stiff in the neck,
'Tis but good riddance.

CHAMBERLAIN.

             One of us must do it.
It might be, if you'd reason with him, ladies,
He would eat something, for I have a notion
That if he brought misfortune on the King,
Or the King's house, we'd be as little thought of
As summer linen when the winter's come.

FIRST GIRL.

But it would be the greater compliment
If Peter'd do it.

SECOND GIRL.

          Reason with him, Peter.
Persuade him to eat; he's such a bag of bones!

SOLDIER.

I'll never trust a woman's word again!
There's nobody that was so loud against him

When he was at the table; now the wind's
    changed,
And you that could not bear his speech or his
    silence,
Would have him there in his old place again;
I do believe you would, but I won't help you.

SECOND GIRL.

Why will you be so hard upon us, Peter?
You know we have turned the common sort
    against us,
And he looks miserable.

FIRST GIRL.

            We cannot dance,
Because no harper will pluck a string for us.

SECOND GIRL.

I cannot sleep with thinking of his face.

FIRST GIRL.

And I love dancing more than anything.

SECOND GIRL.

Do not be hard on us; but yesterday
A woman in the road threw stones at me.
You would not have me stoned?

FIRST GIRL.

May I not dance?

SOLDIER.

I will do nothing. You have put him out,
And now that he is out—well, leave him out.

FIRST GIRL.

Do it for my sake, Peter.

SECOND GIRL.

And for mine.

[*Each girl as she speaks takes* PETER'S *hand
with her right hand, stroking down his arm
with her left. While* SECOND GIRL *is stroking
his arm,* FIRST GIRL *leaves go and gives him
the dish.*

SOLDIER.

Well, well; but not your way. [*To* SEANCHAN.]
Here's meat for you.
It has been carried from too good a table
For men like you, and I am offering it
Because these women have made a fool of me.

[*A pause.*

You mean to starve? You will have none of it?
I'll leave it there, where you can sniff the
    savour.
Snuff it, old hedgehog, and unroll yourself!
But if I were the King, I'd make you do it
With wisps of lighted straw.

SEANCHAN.

                You have rightly named me.
I lie rolled up under the ragged thorns
That are upon the edge of those great waters
Where all things vanish away, and I have
    heard
Murmurs that are the ending of all sound.
I am out of life; I am rolled up, and yet,
Hedgehog although I am, I'll not unroll
For you, King's dog! Go to the King, your
    master.
Crouch down and wag your tail, for it may be
He has nothing now against you, and I think
The stripes of your last beating are all healed.
                [*The* SOLDIER *has drawn his sword.*

CHAMBERLAIN.

[*Striking up sword.*]
Put up your sword, sir; put it up, I say!
The common sort would tear you into pieces
If you but touched him.

SOLDIER.

               If he's to be flattered,
Petted, cajoled, and dandled into humour,
We might as well have left him at the table.
          [Goes to one side sheathing sword.

SEANCHAN.

You must need keep your patience yet awhile,
For I have some few mouthfuls of sweet air
To swallow before I have grown to be as civil
As any other dust.

CHAMBERLAIN.

         You wrong us, Seanchan.
There is none here but holds you in respect;
And if you'd only eat out of this dish,
The King would show how much he honours
    you.
            [Bowing and smiling.
Who could imagine you'd so take to heart
Being put from the high table? I am certain
That you, if you will only think it over,
Will understand that it is men of law,
Leaders of the King's armies, and the like,
That should sit there.

SEANCHAN.

Somebody has deceived you,
Or maybe it was your own eyes that lied,
In making it appear that I was driven
From the King's table. You have driven away
The images of them that weave a dance
By the four rivers in the mountain garden.

CHAMBERLAIN.

You mean we have driven poetry away.
But that's not altogether true, for I,
As you should know, have written poetry.
And often when the table has been cleared,
And candles lighted, the King calls for me,
And I repeat it him.   My poetry
Is not to be compared with yours; but still,
Where I am honoured, poetry is honoured—
In some measure.

SEANCHAN.

If you are a poet,
Cry out that the King's money would not buy,
Nor the high circle consecrate his head,
If poets had never christened gold, and even
The moon's poor daughter, that most whey-
    faced metal,

Precious; and cry out that none alive
Would ride among the arrows with high heart,
Or scatter with an open hand, had not
Our heady craft commended wasteful virtues.
And when that story's finished, shake your coat
Where little jewels gleam on it, and say,
A herdsman, sitting where the pigs had
    trampled,
Made up a song about enchanted kings,
Who were so finely dressed, one fancied them
All fiery, and women by the churn
And children by the hearth caught up the song
And murmured it, until the tailors heard it.

CHAMBERLAIN.

If you would but eat something you'd find out
That you have had these thoughts from lack
    of food,
For hunger makes us feverish.

SEANCHAN.

               Cry aloud,
That when we are driven out we come again
Like a great wind that runs out of the waste
To blow the tables flat; and thereupon
Lie down upon the threshold till the King
Restore to us the ancient right of the poets.

MONK.

You cannot shake him.   I will to the King,
And offer him consolation in his trouble,
For that man there has set his teeth to die.
And being one that hates obedience,
Discipline, and orderliness of life,
I cannot mourn him.

FIRST GIRL.

    'Twas you that stirred it up.
You stirred it up that you might spoil our
  dancing.
Why shouldn't we have dancing?   We're not
  in Lent.
Yet nobody will pipe or play to us;
And they will never do it if he die.
And that is why you are going.

MONK.

      What folly's this?

FIRST GIRL.

Well, if you did not do it, speak to him—
Use your authority; make him obey you.
What harm is there in dancing?

MONK.

      Hush! begone!

Go to the fields and watch the hurley players,
Or any other place you have a mind to.
This is not woman's work.

FIRST GIRL.

                    Come! let's away!
We can do nothing here.

MONK.

                    The pride of the poets!
Dancing, hurling, the country full of noise,
And King and Church neglected.   Seanchan,
I'll take my leave, for you are perishing
Like all that let the wanton imagination
Carry them where it will, and it's not likely
I'll look upon your living face again.

SEANCHAN.

Come nearer, nearer!

MONK.

Have you some last wish?

SEANCHAN.

Stoop down, for I would whisper it in your
    ear.

Has that wild God of yours, that was so wild
When you'd but lately taken the King's pay,
Grown any tamer?   He gave you all much
    trouble.

MONK.

Let go my habit!

SEANCHAN.

                    Have you persuaded him
To chirp between two dishes when the King
Sits down to table?

MONK.

                    Let go my habit, sir!
                    [*Crosses to centre of stage.*

SEANCHAN.

And maybe he has learnt to sing quite softly
Because loud singing would disturb the King,
Who is sitting drowsily among his friends
After the table has been cleared.   Not yet!
    [SEANCHAN *has been dragged some feet clinging
                    to the* MONK's *habit.*

You did not think that hands so full of hunger
Could hold you tightly. They are not civil yet.
I'd know if you have taught him to eat bread

From the King's hand, and perch upon his
    finger.
I think he perches on the King's strong hand.
But it may be that he is still too wild.
You must not weary in your work; a king
Is often weary, and he needs a God
To be a comfort to him.

    [*The* MONK *plucks his habit away and goes into
        palace.* SEANCHAN *holds up his hand as if a
        bird perched upon it. He pretends to stroke
        the bird.*

                        A little God,
With comfortable feathers, and bright eyes.

FIRST GIRL.

There will be no more dancing in our time,
For nobody will play the harp or the fiddle.
Let us away, for we cannot amend it,
And watch the hurley.

SECOND GIRL.

            Hush! he is looking at us.

SEANCHAN.

Yes, yes, go to the hurley, go to the hurley,
Go to the hurley! Gather up your skirts—

Run quickly!   You can remember many love
      songs;
I know it by the light that's in your eyes—
But you'll forget them.   You're fair to look
      upon.
Your feet delight in dancing, and your mouths
In the slow smiling that awakens love.
The mothers that have borne you mated rightly.
They'd little ears as thirsty as your ears
For many love songs. Go to the young men.
Are not the ruddy flesh and the thin flanks
And the broad shoulders worthy of desire?
Go from me! Here is nothing for your eyes.
But it is I that am singing you away—
Singing you to the young men.

> [*The* TWO YOUNG PRINCESSES *come out of palace.*
> *While he has been speaking the* GIRLS *have*
> *shrunk back holding each other's hands.*

FIRST GIRL.

                              Be quiet!
Look who it is has come out of the house.
Princesses, we are for the hurling field.
Will you go there?

FIRST PRINCESS.

            We will go with you, Aileen.

But we must have some words with Seanchan,
For we have come to make him eat and drink.

CHAMBERLAIN.

I will hold out the dish and cup for him
While you are speaking to him of his folly,
If you desire it, Princess.

> [*He has taken dish and cup.*

FIRST PRINCESS.

                No, Finula
Will carry him the dish and I the cup.
We'll offer them ourselves.

> [*They take cup and dish.*

FIRST GIRL.

                They are so gracious;
The dear little Princesses are so gracious.

> [PRINCESS *holds out her hand for* SEANCHAN
> *to kiss it.   He does not move.*

Although she is holding out her hand to him,
He will not kiss it.

FIRST PRINCESS.

        My father bids us say

E

That, though he cannot have you at his table,
You may ask any other thing you like
And he will give it you.   We carry you
With our own hands a dish and cup of wine.

FIRST GIRL.

O, look! he has taken it!   He has taken it!
The dear Princesses!   I have always said
That nobody could refuse them anything.

   [SEANCHAN *takes the cup in one hand. In the
     other he holds for a moment the hand of the*
     PRINCESS.

SEANCHAN.

O long, soft fingers and pale finger-tips,
Well worthy to be laid in a king's hand!
O, you have fair white hands, for it is certain
There is uncommon whiteness in these hands.
But there is something comes into my mind,
Princess. A little while before your birth,
I saw your mother sitting by the road
In a high chair; and when a leper passed,
She pointed him the way into the town.
He lifted up his hand and blessed her hand—
I saw it with my own eyes.   Hold out your
    hands;
I will find out if they are contaminated,

For it has come into my thoughts that maybe
The King has sent me food and drink by hands
That are contaminated.   I would see all your
    hands.
You've eyes of dancers; but hold out your hands,
For it may be there are none sound among you.

   [*The* PRINCESSES *have shrunk back in terror.*

FIRST PRINCESS.

He has called us lepers.

             [SOLDIER *draws sword.*

CHAMBERLAIN.

             He's out of his mind,
And does not know the meaning of what he
    said.

SEANCHAN.

[*Standing up.*]

There's no sound hand among you—no sound
    hand.
Away with you! away with all of you!
You are all lepers!   There is leprosy
Among the plates and dishes that you have
    carried.
And wherefore have you brought me leper's
    wine?

   [*He flings the contents of the cup in their faces.*

There, there!   I have given it to you again.
    And now
Begone, or I will give my curse to you.
You have the leper's blessing, but you think
Maybe the bread will something lack in savour
Unless you mix my curse into the dough.

  [*They go out hurriedly in all directions.* SEAN-
    CHAN *is staggering in the middle of the stage.*

Where did I say the leprosy had come from?
I said it came out of a leper's hand,

Enter CRIPPLES.

And that he walked the highway.   But that's
    folly,
For he was walking up there in the sky.
And there he is even now, with his white
    hand
Thrust out of the blue air, and blessing them
With leprosy.

FIRST CRIPPLE.

      He's pointing at the moon
That's coming out up yonder, and he calls it
Leprous, because the daylight whitens it.

SEANCHAN.

He's holding up his hand above them all—

King, noblemen, princesses—blessing all.
Who could imagine he'd have so much patience?

FIRST CRIPPLE.

[*Clutching the other* CRIPPLE.]
Come out of this!

SECOND CRIPPLE.

[*Pointing to food.*]
　　　　　If you don't need it, sir,
May we not carry some of it away?
　[*They cross towards food and pass in front of*
SEANCHAN.

SEANCHAN.

Who's speaking?　Who are you?

FIRST CRIPPLE.

　　　　　　　Come out of this!

SECOND CRIPPLE.

Have pity on us, that must beg our bread
From table to table throughout the entire
　　world,
And yet be hungry.

SEANCHAN.

But why were you born crooked?
What bad poet did your mothers listen to
That you were born so crooked?

CRIPPLE.

Come away!
Maybe he's cursed the food, and it might kill us.

OTHER CRIPPLE.

Yes, better come away.   [*They go out.*

SEANCHAN.

[*Staggering, and speaking wearily.*]
He has great strength
And great patience to hold his right hand there,
Uplifted, and not wavering about.
He is much stronger than I am, much stronger.
          [*Sinks down on steps.   Enter* MAYOR *and*
FEDELM.

FEDELM.

[*Her finger on her lips.*]
Say nothing!   I will get him out of this
Before I have said a word of food and drink;
For while he is on this threshold and can hear,

It may be, the voices that made mock of him,
He would not listen. I'd be alone with him.

> [MAYOR *goes out.*   FEDELM *goes to* SEANCHAN
>   *and kneels before him.*

Seanchan! Seanchan!

> [*He remains looking into the sky.*

         Can you not hear me, Seanchan?
It is myself.

> [*He looks at her, dreamily at first, then takes
>   her hand.*

SEANCHAN.

      Is this your hand, Fedelm?
I have been looking at another hand
That is up yonder.

FEDELM.

I have come for you.

SEANCHAN.

Fedelm, I did not know that you were here.

FEDELM.

And can you not remember that I promised
That I would come and take you home with me

When I'd the harvest in? And now I've come,
And you must come away, and come on the
    instant.

SEANCHAN.

Yes, I will come.   But is the harvest in?
This air has got a summer taste in it.

FEDELM.

But is not the wild middle of the summer
A better time to marry? Come with me now!

SEANCHAN.

[*Seizing her by both wrists.*]
Who taught you that? For it's a certainty,
Although I never knew it till last night,
That marriage, because it is the height of life,
Can only be accomplished to the full
In the high days of the year.   I lay awake:
There had come a frenzy into the light of the
    stars,
And they were coming nearer, and I knew
All in a minute they were about to marry
Clods out upon the ploughlands, to beget
A mightier race than any that has been.
But some that are within there made a noise,
And frighted them away.

FEDELM.

Come with me now!
We have far to go, and daylight's running out.

SEANCHAN.

The stars had come so near me that I caught
Their singing. It was praise of that great race
That would be haughty, mirthful, and white-
    bodied,
With a high head, and open hand, and how,
Laughing, it would take the mastery of the
    world.

FEDELM.

But you will tell me all about their songs
When we're at home. You have need of rest
    and care,
And I can give them you when we're at home.
And therefore let us hurry, and get us home.

SEANCHAN.

It's certain that there is some trouble here,
Although it's gone out of my memory.
And I would get away from it. Give me your
    help.   [*Trying to rise.*
But why are not my pupils here to help me?
Go, call my pupils, for I need their help.

FEDELM.

Come with me now, and I will send for them,
For I have a great room that's full of beds
I can make ready; and there is a smooth lawn
Where they can play at hurley and sing poems
Under an apple-tree.

SEANCHAN.

           I know that place:
An apple-tree, and a smooth level lawn
Where the young men can sway their hurley
    sticks.
          [*Sings.*]
    The four rivers that run there,
    Through well-mown level ground,
    Have come out of a blessed well
    That is all bound and wound
    By the great roots of an apple,
    And all the fowl of the air
    Have gathered in the wide branches
    And keep singing there.
   [FEDELM, *troubled, has covered her eyes with*
    her hands.

FEDELM.

No, there are not four rivers, and those rhymes
Praise Adam's paradise.

SEANCHAN.

                    I can remember now,
It's out of a poem I made long ago
About the Garden in the East of the World,
And how spirits in the images of birds
Crowd in the branches of old Adam's crab-
        tree.
They come before me now, and dig in the fruit
With so much gluttony, and are so drunk
With that harsh wholesome savour, that their
        feathers
Are clinging one to another with the juice.
But you would lead me to some friendly place,
And I would go there quickly.

FEDELM.

[*Helping him to rise.*]

                    Come with me.
[*He walks slowly, supported by her, till he
    comes to table.*

SEANCHAN.

But why am I so weak? Have I been ill?
Sweetheart, why is it that I am so weak?
                    [*Sinks on to seat.*

FEDELM.

[Goes to table.]

I'll dip this piece of bread into the wine,
For that will make you stronger for the journey.

SEANCHAN.

Yes, give me bread and wine; that's what I
    want,
For it is hunger that is gnawing me.
    [He takes bread from FEDELM, *hesitates, and
        then thrusts it back into her hand.*
But, no; I must not eat it.

FEDELM.

                        Eat, Seanchan.
For if you do not eat it you will die.

SEANCHAN.

Why did you give me food?   Why did you
    come?
For had I not enough to fight against
Without your coming?

FEDELM.

                Eat this little crust,
Seanchan, if you have any love for me.

SEANCHAN.

I must not eat it—but that's beyond your wit.
Child! child! I must not eat it, though I die.

FEDELM.

[*Passionately.*]

You do not know what love is; for if you loved,
You would put every other thought away.
But you have never loved me.

SEANCHAN.

[*Seizing her by wrist.*]

                              You, a child,
Who have but seen a man out of the window,
Tell me that I know nothing about love,
And that I do not love you!   Did I not say
There was a frenzy in the light of the stars
All through the livelong night, and that the
        night
Was full of marriages?   But that fight's over,
And all that's done with, and I have to die.

FEDELM.

[*Throwing her arms about him.*]

I will not be put from you, although I think
I had not grudged it you if some great lady,

If the King's daughter, had set out your bed.
I will not give you up to death; no, no!
And are not these white arms and this soft neck
Better than the brown earth?

SEANCHAN.

[*Struggling to disengage himself.*]

Begone from me!
There's treachery in those arms and in that
    voice.
They're all against me.   Why do you linger
    there?
How long must I endure the sight of you?

FEDELM.

O, Seanchan! Seanchan!

SEANCHAN.

[*Rising.*]

Go where you will,
So it be out of sight and out of mind.
I cast you from me like an old torn cap,
A broken shoe, a glove without a finger,
A crooked penny; whatever is most worthless.

FEDELM.

[*Bursts into tears.*]

O, do not drive me from you!

SEANCHAN.

[*Takes her in his arms.*]

What did I say,
My dove of the woods? I was about to curse
     you.
It was a frenzy.   I'll unsay it all.
But you must go away.

FEDELM.

Let me be near you.
I will obey like any married wife.
Let me but lie before your feet.

SEANCHAN.

Come nearer.
[*Kisses her.*

If I had eaten when you bid me, sweetheart,
The kiss of multitudes in times to come
Had been the poorer.
     [*Enter* KING *from palace, followed by the two*
     PRINCESSES.

KING.
[*To* FEDELM.]

Has he eaten yet?

FEDELM.

No, King, and will not till you have restored
The right of the poets.

KING.

[*Coming down and standing before* SEANCHAN.]

                      Seanchan, you have refused
Everybody that I have sent, and now
I come to you myself; and I have come
To bid you put your pride as far away
As I have put my pride.   I had your love
Not a great while ago, and now you have
    planned
To put a voice by every cottage fire,
And in the night when no one sees who cries,
To cry against me till my throne has crumbled.
And yet if I give way I must offend
My courtiers and nobles till they, too,
Strike at the crown.   What would you have
    of me?

SEANCHAN.

When did the poets promise safety, King?

KING.

Seanchan, I bring you bread in my own hands,

And bid you eat because of all these reasons,
And for this further reason, that I love you.

[SEANCHAN *pushes bread away, with* FEDELM'S
hand.

You have refused it, Seanchan?

SEANCHAN.

We have refused it.

KING.

I have been patient, though I am a king,
And have the means to force you.   But that's
    ended,
And I am but a king, and you a subject.
Nobles and courtiers, bring the poets hither;

[*Enter* COURT LADIES, MONK, SOLDIER, CHAM-
BERLAIN, *and* COURTIERS *with* PUPILS, *who
have halters round their necks.*

For you can have your way.   I that was man,
With a man's heart, am now all king again,
Remembering that the seed I come of, though
A hundred kings have sown it and resown it,
Has neither trembled nor shrunk backward yet
Because of the hard business of a king.
Speak to your master; beg your life of him;
Show him the halter that is round your necks.
If his heart's set upon it, he may die;

F

But you shall all die with him. [*Goes up steps.*
                              Beg your lives!
Begin, for you have little time to lose.
Begin it, you that are the oldest pupil.

OLDEST PUPIL.

Die, Seanchan, and proclaim the right of the
    poets.

KING.

Silence! you are as crazy as your master.
But that young boy, that seems the youngest
    of you,
I'd have him speak. Kneel down before him,
    boy;
Hold up your hands to him, that you may pluck
That milky-coloured neck out of the noose.

YOUNGEST PUPIL.

Die, Seanchan, and proclaim the right of the
    poets.

OLDEST PUPIL.

Gather the halters up into your hands
And drive us where you will, for in all things,
But in our Art, we are obedient.

    [*They hold the ends of the halter towards the*
        KING. *The* KING *comes slowly down steps.*

KING.

Kneel down, kneel down; he has the greater
  power.
There is no power but has its root in his—
I understand it now.   There is no power
But his that can withhold the crown or give it,
Or make it reverend in the eyes of men,
And therefore I have laid it in his hands,
And I will do his will.

[*He has put the crown into* SEANCHAN'S *hands.*

SEANCHAN.

[*Who has been assisted to rise by his pupils.*]
                    O crown! O crown!
It is but right the hands that made the crown
In the old time should give it where they please.

[*He places the crown on the* KING'S *head.*

O silver trumpets! Be you lifted up,
And cry to the great race that is to come.
Long-throated swans, amid the waves of Time,
Sing loudly, for beyond the wall of the world
It waits, and it may hear and come to us.

[*The* PUPILS *blow a trumpet blast.*

ON BAILE'S STRAND

To William Fay

BECAUSE OF THE BEAUTIFUL PHANTASY OF HIS
PLAYING IN THE CHARACTER OF
THE FOOL

PERSONS IN THE PLAY

A FOOL

A BLIND MAN

CUCHULAIN, *King of Muirthemne*

CONCHUBAR, *High King of Ulad*

A YOUNG MAN, *Son of Cuchulain*

KINGS AND SINGING WOMEN

ON BAILE'S STRAND

*A great hall at Dundealgan, not 'Cuchulain's great
ancient house' but an assembly house nearer to
the sea. A big door at the back, and through
the door misty light as of sea mist. There are
many chairs and one long bench. One of these
chairs, which is towards the front of the stage,
is bigger than the others. Somewhere at the back
there is a table with flagons of ale upon it and
drinking-horns. There is a small door at one
side of the hall. A* FOOL *and* BLIND MAN, *both
ragged, come in through the door at the back.
The* BLIND MAN *leans upon a staff.*

FOOL.

WHAT a clever man you are though you are
blind! There's nobody with two eyes in his
head that is as clever as you are. Who but
you could have thought that the henwife sleeps
every day a little at noon? I would never be
able to steal anything if you didn't tell me where

to look for it.   And what a good cook you are !
You take the fowl out of my hands after I have
stolen it and plucked it, and you put it into the
big pot at the fire there, and I can go out and
run races with the witches at the edge of the
waves and get an appetite, and when I've got
it, there's the hen waiting inside for me, done
to the turn.

BLIND MAN.

[*Who is feeling about with his stick.*]
Done to the turn.

FOOL.

[*Putting his arm round* BLIND MAN's *neck.*]
Come now, I'll have a leg and you'll have a
leg, and we'll draw lots for the wish-bone.   I'll
be praising you, I'll be praising you, while
we're eating it, for your good plans and for
your good cooking.   There's nobody in the
world like you, Blind Man.   Come, come. Wait
a minute.   I shouldn't have closed the door.
There are some that look for me, and I wouldn't
like them not to find me.   Don't tell it to any-
body, Blind Man.   There are some that follow
me.   Boann herself out of the river and Fand
out of the deep sea.   Witches they are, and
they come by in the wind, and they cry, 'Give

a kiss, Fool, give a kiss,' that's what they cry.
That's wide enough. All the witches can come
in now. I wouldn't have them beat at the
door and say : 'Where is the Fool? Why has
he put a lock on the door?' Maybe they'll
hear the bubbling of the pot and come in and
sit on the ground. But we won't give them
any of the fowl. Let them go back to the sea,
let them go back to the sea.

BLIND MAN.

[*Feeling legs of big chair with his hands.*]

Ah! [*Then, in a louder voice as he feels the
back of it.*] Ah—ah—

FOOL.

Why do you say 'Ah-ah'?

BLIND MAN.

I know the big chair. It is to-day the
High King Conchubar is coming. They have
brought out his chair. He is going to be
Cuchulain's master in earnest from this day
out. It is that he's coming for.

FOOL.

He must be a great man to be Cuchulain's
master.

BLIND MAN.

So he is. He is a great man. He is over all
the rest of the kings of Ireland.

FOOL.

Cuchulain's master! I thought Cuchulain
could do anything he liked.

BLIND MAN.

So he did, so he did. But he ran too wild,
and Conchubar is coming to-day to put an oath
upon him that will stop his rambling and make
him as biddable as a house-dog and keep him
always at his hand. He will sit in this chair
and put the oath upon him.

FOOL.

How will he do that?

BLIND MAN.

You have no wits to understand such things.
[*The* BLIND MAN *has got into the chair.*] He
will sit up in this chair and he'll say : 'Take
the oath, Cuchulain. I bid you take the oath.
Do as I tell you. What are your wits com-
pared with mine, and what are your riches
compared with mine? And what sons have
you to pay your debts and to put a stone over

you when you die? Take the oath, I tell you. Take a strong oath.'

FOOL.

[*Crumpling himself up and whining.*]

I will not. I'll take no oath. I want my dinner.

BLIND MAN.

Hush, hush! It is not done yet.

FOOL.

You said it was done to a turn.

BLIND MAN.

Did I, now? Well, it might be done, and not done. The wings might be white, but the legs might be red. The flesh might stick hard to the bones and not come away in the teeth. But, believe me, Fool, it will be well done before you put your teeth in it.

FOOL.

My teeth are growing long with the hunger.

BLIND MAN.

I'll tell you a story—the kings have story-tellers while they are waiting for their dinner

—I will tell you a story with a fight in it, a story with a champion in it, and a ship and a queen's son that has his mind set on killing somebody that you and I know.

FOOL.

Who is that? Who is he coming to kill?

BLIND MAN.

Wait, now, till you hear. When you were stealing the fowl, I was lying in a hole in the sand, and I heard three men coming with a shuffling sort of noise. They were wounded and groaning.

FOOL.

Go on. Tell me about the fight.

BLIND MAN.

There had been a fight, a great fight, a tremendous great fight. A young man had landed on the shore, the guardians of the shore had asked his name, and he had refused to tell it, and he had killed one, and others had run away.

FOOL.

That's enough. Come on now to the fowl. I wish it was bigger. I wish it was as big as a goose.

BLIND MAN.

Hush! I haven't told you all. I know who
that young man is. I heard the men who were
running away say he had red hair, that he had
come from Aoife's country, that he was coming
to kill Cuchulain.

FOOL.

Nobody can do that.
[*To a tune.*]
Cuchulain has killed kings,
Kings and sons of kings,
Dragons out of the water,
And witches out of the air,
Banachas and Bonachas and people of the woods.

BLIND MAN.

Hush! hush!

FOOL.

[*Still singing.*]
Witches that steal the milk,
Fomor that steal the children,
Hags that have heads like hares,
Hares that have claws like witches,
All riding a-cockhorse
[*Spoken.*]
Out of the very bottom of the bitter black north.

BLIND MAN.

Hush, I say !

FOOL.

Does Cuchulain know that he is coming to kill him?

BLIND MAN.

How would he know that with his head in the clouds? He doesn't care for common fighting. Why would he put himself out, and nobody in it but that young man? Now, if it were a white fawn that might turn into a queen before morning—

FOOL.

Come to the fowl. I wish it was as big as a pig; a fowl with goose grease and pig's crackling.

BLIND MAN.

No hurry, no hurry. I know whose son it is. I wouldn't tell anybody else, but I will tell you,—a secret is better to you than your dinner. You like being told secrets.

FOOL.

Tell me the secret.

BLIND MAN.

That young man is Aoife's son. I am sure it is Aoife's son, it flows in upon me that it is Aoife's son. You have often heard me talking of Aoife, the great woman-fighter Cuchulain got the mastery over in the north?

FOOL.

I know, I know. She is one of those cross queens that live in hungry Scotland.

BLIND MAN.

I am sure it is her son. I was in Aoife's country for a long time.

FOOL.

That was before you were blinded for putting a curse upon the wind.

BLIND MAN.

There was a boy in her house that had her own red colour on him and everybody said he was to be brought up to kill Cuchulain, that she hated Cuchulain. She used to put a helmet on a pillar-stone and call it Cuchulain and set him casting at it. There is a step outside— Cuchulain's step.

G

[CUCHULAIN *passes by in the mist outside the big door.*

FOOL.

Where is Cuchulain going?

BLIND MAN.

He is going to meet Conchubar that has bidden him to take the oath.

FOOL.

Ah, an oath, Blind Man. How can I remember so many things at once? Who is going to take an oath?

BLIND MAN.

Cuchulain is going to take an oath to Conchubar who is High King.

FOOL.

What a mix-up you make of everything, Blind Man. You were telling me one story, and now you are telling me another story . . . How can I get the hang of it at the end if you mix everything at the beginning? Wait till I settle it out. There now, there's Cuchulain [*he points to one foot*], and there is the young man [*he points to the other foot*] that is coming to kill him, and Cuchulain doesn't know. But

where's Conchubar? [*Takes bag from side.*]
That's Conchubar with all his riches—Cuchu-
lain, young man, Conchubar—And where's
Aoife? [*Throws up cap.*]   There is Aoife, high
up on the mountains in high hungry Scotland.
Maybe it is not true after all.   Maybe it was
your own making up.   It's many a time you
cheated me before with your lies.   Come to the
cooking-pot, my stomach is pinched and rusty.
Would you have it to be creaking like a gate?

BLIND MAN.

I tell you it's true.   And more than that is
true.   If you listen to what I say, you'll forget
your stomach.

FOOL.

I won't.

BLIND MAN.

Listen.   I know who the young man's father
is, but I won't say.   I would be afraid to say.
Ah, Fool, you would forget everything if you
could know who the young man's father is.

FOOL.

Who is it?   Tell me now quick, or I'll shake
you.   Come, out with it, or I'll shake you.

[*A murmur of voices in the distance.*

BLIND MAN.

Wait, wait. There's somebody coming . . .
It is Cuchulain is coming. He's coming back
with the High King. Go and ask Cuchulain.
He'll tell you. It's little you'll care about the
cooking-pot when you have asked Cuchulain
that . . .

[BLIND MAN *goes out by side door.*

FOOL.

I'll ask him. Cuchulain will know. He was
in Aoife's country. [*Goes up stage.*] I'll ask him.
[*Turns and goes down stage.*] But, no. I won't
ask him, I would be afraid. [*Going up again.*]
Yes, I will ask him. What harm in asking?
The Blind Man said I was to ask him. [*Going
down.*] No, no. I'll not ask him. He might kill
me. I have but killed hens and geese and pigs.
He has killed kings. [*Goes up again almost to big
door.*] Who says I'm afraid? I'm not afraid.
I'm no coward. I'll ask him. No, no, Cuchu-
lain, I'm not going to ask you.

> He has killed kings,
> Kings and the sons of kings,
> Dragons out of the water,
> And witches out of the air,
Banachas and Bonachas and people of the woods.

[FOOL *goes out by side door, the last words being heard*
     outside. CUCHULAIN *and* CONCHUBAR *enter*
     through the big door at the back. While they
     are still outside, CUCHULAIN'S *voice is heard*
     raised in anger. He is a dark man, something
     over forty years of age. CONCHUBAR *is much*
     older and carries a long staff, elaborately
     carved, or with an elaborate gold handle.

CUCHULAIN.

Because I have killed men without your bidding
And have rewarded others at my own pleasure,
Because of half a score of trifling things
You'd lay this oath upon me, and now—and now
You add another pebble to the heap.
And I must be your man, well-nigh your bonds-
     man,
Because a youngster out of Aoife's country
Has found the shore ill-guarded.

CONCHUBAR.

                         He came to land
While you were somewhere out of sight and
     hearing,
Hunting or dancing with your wild com-
     panions.

CUCHULAIN.

He can be driven out. I'll not be bound.

I'll dance or hunt, or quarrel or make love,
Wherever and whenever I've a mind to.
If time had not put water in your blood,
You never would have thought it.

CONCHUBAR.

                                        I would leave
A strong and settled country to my children.

CUCHULAIN.

And I must be obedient in all things;
Give up my will to yours; go where you please;
Come when you call; sit at the council-board
Among the unshapely bodies of old men.
I whose mere name has kept this country safe,
I that in early days have driven out
Maeve of Cruachan and the northern pirates,
The hundred kings of Sorcha, and the kings
Out of the Garden in the East of the World.
Must I, that held you on the throne when all
Had pulled you from it, swear obedience
As if I were some cattle-raising king?
Are my shins speckled with the heat of the fire,
Or have my hands no skill but to make figures
Upon the ashes with a stick?   Am I
So slack and idle that I need a whip
Before I serve you?

CONCHUBAR.

No, no whip, Cuchulain,
But every day my children come and say :
'This man is growing harder to endure.
How can we be at safety with this man
That nobody can buy or bid or bind?
We shall be at his mercy when you are gone;
He burns the earth as if he were a fire,
And time can never touch him.'

CUCHULAIN.

And so the tale
Grows finer yet; and I am to obey
Whatever child you set upon the throne,
As if it were yourself!

CONCHUBAR.

Most certainly.
I am High King, my son shall be High King;
And you for all the wildness of your blood,
And though your father came out of the sun,
Are but a little king and weigh but light
In anything that touches government,
If put into the balance with my children.

CUCHULAIN.

It's well that we should speak our minds out
    plainly,

For when we die we shall be spoken of
In many countries.   We in our young days
Have seen the heavens like a burning cloud
Brooding upon the world, and being more
Than men can be now that cloud's lifted up,
We should be the more truthful.   Conchubar,
I do not like your children—they have no pith,
No marrow in their bones, and will lie soft
Where you and I lie hard.

CONCHUBAR.

You rail at them
Because you have no children of your own.

CUCHULAIN.

I think myself most lucky that I leave
No pallid ghost or mockery of a man
To drift and mutter in the corridors,
Where I have laughed and sung.

CONCHUBAR.

That is not true,
For all your boasting of the truth between us;
For, there is no man having house and lands,
That have been in the one family
And called by the one name for centuries,
But is made miserable if he know
They are to pass into a stranger's keeping,
As yours will pass.

CUCHULAIN.

         The most of men feel that,
But you and I leave names upon the harp.

CONCHUBAR.

You play with arguments as lawyers do,
And put no heart in them. I know your thoughts,
For we have slept under the one cloak and drunk
From the one wine cup. I know you to the bone.
I have heard you cry, aye in your very sleep,
'I have no son,' and with such bitterness
That I have gone upon my knees and prayed
That it might be amended.

CUCHULAIN.

         For you thought
That I should be as biddable as others
Had I their reason for it; but that's not true,
For I would need a weightier argument
Than one that marred me in the copying,
As I have that clean hawk out of the air
That, as men say, begot this body of mine
Upon a mortal woman.

CONCHUBAR.

         Now as ever
You mock at every reasonable hope,
And would have nothing, or impossible things.
What eye has ever looked upon the child
Would satisfy a mind like that?

CUCHULAIN.

I would leave
My house and name to none that would not face
Even myself in battle.

CONCHUBAR.

Being swift of foot,
And making light of every common chance,
You should have overtaken on the hills
Some daughter of the air, or on the shore
A daughter of the Country-under-Wave.

CUCHULAIN.

I am not blasphemous.

CONCHUBAR.

Yet you despise
Our queens, and would not call a child your own,
If one of them had borne him.

CUCHULAIN.

I have not said it.

CONCHUBAR.

Ah! I remember I have heard you boast,
When the ale was in your blood, that there
was one

In Scotland, where you had learnt the trade of
    war,
That had a stone-pale cheek and red-brown
    hair.
And that although you had loved other women,
You'd sooner that fierce woman of the camp
.Bore you a son than any queen among them.

CUCHULAIN.

You call her a 'fierce woman of the camp,'
For having lived among the spinning-wheels,
You'd have no woman near that would not say,
'Ah! how wise!' 'What will you have for
    supper?'
'What shall I wear that I may please you, sir?'
And keep that humming through the day and
    night
Forever. A fierce woman of the camp!
But I am getting angry about nothing.
You have never seen her. Ah! Conchubar, had
    you seen her
With that high, laughing, turbulent head of hers
Thrown backward, and the bow-string at her
    ear,
Or sitting at the fire with those grave eyes
Full of good counsel as it were with wine,
Or when love ran through all the lineaments
Of her wild body—although she had no child,

None other had all beauty, queen, or lover,
Or was so fitted to give birth to kings.

CONCHUBAR.

There's nothing I can say but drifts you farther
From the one weighty matter. That very
    woman—
For I know well that you are praising Aoife—
Now hates you and will leave no subtilty
Unknotted that might run into a noose
About your throat, no army in idleness
That might bring ruin on this land you serve.

CUCHULAIN.

No wonder in that, no wonder at all in that.
I never have known love but as a kiss
In the mid-battle, and a difficult truce
Of oil and water, candles and dark night,
Hillside and hollow, the hot-footed sun,
And the cold, sliding, slippery-footed moon—
A brief forgiveness between opposites
That have been hatreds for three times the age
Of this long-'stablished ground.

CONCHUBAR.

                                Listen to me.
Aoife makes war on us, and every day

Our enemies grow greater and beat the walls
More bitterly, and you within the walls
Are every day more turbulent; and yet,
When I would speak about these things, your
    fancy
Runs as it were a swallow on the wind.

[*Outside the door in the blue light of the sea
mist are many old and young* KINGS; *amongst
them are three* WOMEN, *two of whom carry a
bowl full of fire. The third, in what follows,
puts from time to time fragrant herbs into the
fire so that it flickers up into brighter flame.*

Look at the door and what men gather there—
Old counsellors that steer the land with me,
And younger kings, the dancers and harp-
    players
That follow in your tumults, and all these
Are held there by the one anxiety.
Will you be bound into obedience
And so make this land safe for them and theirs?
You are but half a king and I but half;
I need your might of hand and burning heart,
And you my wisdom.

                    CUCHULAIN.
            [*Going near to door.*]
                        Nestlings of a high nest,
Hawks that have followed me into the air

And looked upon the sun, we'll out of this
And sail upon the wind once more. This king
Would have me take an oath to do his will,
And having listened to his tune from morning,
I will no more of it. (Run to the stable
And set the horses to the chariot-pole,
And send a messenger to the harp-players.
We'll find a level place among the woods,
And dance awhile.

A YOUNG KING.

Cuchulain, take the oath.
There is none here that would not have you
    take it.

CUCHULAIN.

You'd have me take it ? Are you of one mind ?

THE KINGS.

All, all, all, all !

A YOUNG KING.

Do what the High King bids you.

CONCHUBAR.

There is not one but dreads this turbulence
Now that they're settled men.

CUCHULAIN.

     Are you so changed,
Or have I grown more dangerous of late?
But that's not it. I understand it all.
It's you that have changed. You've wives and
  children now,
And for that reason cannot follow one
That lives like a bird's flight from tree to tree.—
It's time the years put water in my blood
And drowned the wildness of it, for all's changed,
But that unchanged.—I'll take what oath you
  will:
The moon, the sun, the water, light, or air,
I do not care how binding.

CONCHUBAR.

     On this fire
That has been lighted from your hearth and
  mine;
The older men shall be my witnesses,
The younger, yours. The holders of the fire
Shall purify the thresholds of the house
With waving fire, and shut the outer door,
According to the custom; and sing rhyme
That has come down from the old law-makers
To blow the witches out. Considering
That the wild will of man could be oath-bound,
But that a woman's could not, they bid us sing

Against the will of woman at its wildest
In the shape-changers that run upon the wind.

[CONCHUBAR *has gone on to his throne.*]

THE WOMEN.

[*They sing in a very low voice after the first few
    words so that the others all but drown their
    words.*

May this fire have driven out
The shape-changers that can put
Ruin on a great king's house
Until all be ruinous.
Names whereby a man has known
The threshold and the hearthstone,
Gather on the wind and drive
The women, none can kiss and thrive,
For they are but whirling wind,
Out of memory and mind.
They would make a prince decay
With light images of clay,
Planted in the running wave;
Or, for many shapes they have,
They would change them into hounds,
Until he had died of his wounds,
Though the change were but a whim;
Or they'd hurl a spell at him,
That he follow with desire

Bodies that can never tire,
Or grow kind, for they anoint
All their bodies, joint by joint,
With a miracle-working juice
That is made out of the grease
Of the ungoverned unicorn.
But the man is thrice forlorn,
Emptied, ruined, wracked, and lost,
That they follow, for at most
They will give him kiss for kiss;
While they murmur, 'After this
Hatred may be sweet to the taste.'
Those wild hands that have embraced
All his body can but shove
At the burning wheel of love,
Till the side of hate comes up.
Therefore in this ancient cup
May the sword-blades drink their fill
Of the homebrew there, until
They will have for masters none
But the threshold and hearthstone.

CUCHULAIN.

[*Speaking, while they are singing.*]

I'll take and keep this oath, and from this day
I shall be what you please, my chicks, my
    nestlings.

H

Yet I had thought you were of those that
    praised
Whatever life could make the pulse run quickly,
Even though it were brief, and that you held
That a free gift was better than a forced.—
But that's all over.—I will keep it, too.
I never gave a gift and took it again.
If the wild horse should break the chariot-pole,
It would be punished.   Should that be in the oath?

    [*Two of the* WOMEN, *still singing, crouch in front
    of him holding the bowl over their heads.   He
    spreads his hands over the flame.*

I swear to be obedient in all things
To Conchubar, and to uphold his children.

CONCHUBAR.

We are one being, as these flames are one:
I give my wisdom, and I take your strength.
Now thrust the swords into the flame, and pray
That they may serve the threshold and the
    hearthstone
With faithful service.

    [*The* KINGS *kneel in a semicircle before the two*
    WOMEN *and* CUCHULAIN, *who thrusts his sword
    into the flame.   They all put the points of their
    swords into the flame.   The third* WOMAN *is at
    the back near the big door.*

CUCHULAIN.

O pure, glittering ones
That should be more than wife or friend or
mistress,
Give us the enduring will, the unquenchable
hope,
The friendliness of the sword!—

[*The song grows louder, and the last words ring
out clearly. There is a loud knocking at the
door, and a cry of* 'Open! open!'

CONCHUBAR.

Some king that has been loitering on the way.
Open the door, for I would have all know
That the oath's finished and Cuchulain bound,
And that the swords are drinking up the flame.

[*The door is opened by the third* WOMAN, *and a*
YOUNG MAN *with a drawn sword enters.*

YOUNG MAN.

I am of Aoife's army.

[*The* KINGS *rush towards him.* CUCHULAIN
throws himself between.

CUCHULAIN.

Put up your swords.
He is but one. Aoife is far away.

YOUNG MAN.

I have come alone into the midst of you
To weigh this sword against Cuchulain's sword.

CONCHUBAR.

And are you noble? for if of common seed,
You cannot weigh your sword against his sword
But in mixed battle.

YOUNG MAN.

          I am under bonds
To tell my name to no man; but it's noble.

CONCHUBAR.

But I would know your name and not your
    bonds.
You cannot speak in the Assembly House,
If you are not noble.

FIRST OLD KING.

          Answer the High King!

YOUNG MAN.

I will give no other proof than the hawk gives—
That it's no sparrow!
   [*He is silent for a moment, then speaks to all.*]
          Yet look upon me, kings.
I, too, am of that ancient seed, and carry
The signs about this body and in these bones.

CUCHULAIN.

To have shown the hawk's grey feather is
    enough,
And you speak highly, too. Give me that
    helmet.
I'd thought they had grown weary sending
    champions.
That sword and belt will do. This fighting's
    welcome.
The High King there has promised me his
    wisdom;
But the hawk's sleepy till its well-beloved
Cries out amid the acorns, or it has seen
Its enemy like a speck upon the sun.
What's wisdom to the hawk, when that clear eye
Is burning nearer up in the high air?

[*Looks hard at* YOUNG MAN; *then comes down
    steps and grasps* YOUNG MAN *by shoulder.*

Hither into the light.
[*To* CONCHUBAR.]   The very tint
Of her that I was speaking of but now.
Not a pin's difference.
[*To* YOUNG MAN.]   You are from the North
Where there are many that have that tint of
    hair—
Red-brown, the light red-brown. Come nearer,
    boy,

For I would have another look at you.
There's more likeness—a pale, a stone-pale
    cheek.
What brought you, boy? Have you no fear of
    death?

YOUNG MAN.

Whether I live or die is in the gods' hands.

CUCHULAIN.

That is all words, all words; a young man's talk.
I am their plough, their harrow, their very
    strength;
For he that's in the sun begot this body
Upon a mortal woman, and I have heard tell
It seemed as if he had outrun the moon;
That he must follow always through waste
    heaven,
He loved so happily.   He'll be but slow
To break a tree that was so sweetly planted.
Let's see that arm.   I'll see it if I choose.
That arm had a good father and a good mother,
But it is not like this.

YOUNG MAN.

                    You are mocking me;
You think I am not worthy to be fought.
But I'll not wrangle but with this talkative
    knife.

CUCHULAIN.

Put up your sword; I am not mocking you.
I'd have you for my friend, but if it's not
Because you have a hot heart and a cold eye,
I cannot tell the reason.
[*To* CONCHUBAR.] He has got her fierceness,
And nobody is as fierce as those pale women.
But I will keep him with me, Conchubar,
That he may set my memory upon her
When the day's fading.—You will stop with us,
And we will hunt the deer and the wild bulls;
And, when we have grown weary, light our
       fires
Between the wood and water, or on some moun-
       tain
Where the shape-changers of the morning come.
The High King there would make a mock of
       me
Because I did not take a wife among them.
Why do you hang your head?   It's a good life:
The head grows prouder in the light of the
       dawn,
And friendship thickens in the murmuring dark
Where the spare hazels meet the wool-white
       foam.
But I can see there's no more need for words
And that you'll be my friend from this day out.

CONCHUBAR.

He has come hither not in his own name
But in Queen Aoife's, and has challenged us
In challenging the foremost man of us all.

CUCHULAIN.

Well, well, what matter?

CONCHUBAR.

            You think it does not matter;
And that a fancy lighter than the air,
A whim of the moment has more matter in it.
For having none that shall reign after you,
You cannot think as I do, who would leave
A throne too high for insult.

CUCHULAIN.

                Let your children
Re-mortar their inheritance, as we have,
And put more muscle on.—I'll give you gifts,
But I'd have something too—that arm-ring,
    boy.
We'll have this quarrel out when you are older.

YOUNG MAN.

There is no man I'd sooner have my friend
Than you, whose name has gone about the
    world

CUCHULAIN.

Back! back! Put up your swords! Put up
your swords!
There's none alive that shall accept a challenge
I have refused. Laegaire, put up your sword!

YOUNG MAN.

No, let them come. If they've a mind for it,
I'll try it out with any two together.

CUCHULAIN.

That's spoken as I'd have spoken it at your age.
But you are in my house. Whatever man
Would fight with you shall fight it out with
me.
They're dumb, they're dumb. How many of
you would meet   [Draws sword.
This mutterer, this old whistler, this sand-
piper,
This edge that's greyer than the tide, this mouse
That's gnawing at the timbers of the world,
This, this—— Boy, I would meet them all in
arms
If I'd a son like you. He would avenge me
When I have withstood for the last time the
men
Whose fathers, brothers, sons, and friends I
have killed

Upholding Conchubar, when the four provinces
Have gathered with the ravens over them.
But I'd need no avenger.   You and I
Would scatter them like water from a dish.

YOUNG MAN.

We'll stand by one another from this out.
Here is the ring.

CUCHULAIN.

No, turn and turn about.
But my turn's first because I am the older.

[Spreading out cloak.

Nine queens out of the Country-under-Wave
Have woven it with the fleeces of the sea
And they were long embroidering at it.—Boy,
If I had fought my father, he'd have killed me.
As certainly as if I had a son
And fought with him, I should be deadly to
    him;
For the old fiery fountains are far off
And every day there is less heat o' the blood.

CONCHUBAR.

[In a loud voice.]
No more of this. I will not have this friendship.
Cuchulain is my man, and I forbid it.
He shall not go unfought, for I myself—

CUCHULAIN.

I will not have it.

CONCHUBAR.

You lay commands on me?

CUCHULAIN.

[*Seizing* CONCHUBAR.]

You shall not stir, High King. I'll hold you
    there.

CONCHUBAR.

Witchcraft has maddened you.

THE KINGS [*shouting*].

Yes, witchcraft! witchcraft!

FIRST OLD KING.

Some witch has worked upon your mind,
    Cuchulain.
The head of that young man seemed like a
    woman's
You'd had a fancy for.   Then of a sudden
You laid your hands on the High King himself!

CUCHULAIN.

And laid my hands on the High King himself?

CONCHUBAR.

Some witch is floating in the air above us.

CUCHULAIN.

Yes, witchcraft, witchcraft!   Witches of the
    air!   [*To* YOUNG MAN.
Why did you?   Who was it set you to this
    work?
Out, out! I say, for now it's sword on sword!

YOUNG MAN.

But . . . but I did not.

CUCHULAIN.

                    Out, I say, out, out!

[YOUNG MAN *goes out followed by* CUCHULAIN.
    The KINGS *follow them out with confused cries,
    and words one can hardly hear because of the
    noise. Some cry,* 'Quicker, quicker!' 'Why
    are you so long at the door?' 'We'll be
    too late!' 'Have they begun to fight?'
    and so on; and one, it may be, 'I saw him
    fight with Ferdia!' *Their voices drown each
    other. The three women are left alone.*

FIRST WOMAN.

I have seen, I have seen!

SECOND WOMAN.
> What do you cry aloud?

FIRST WOMAN.

The ever-living have shown me what's to come.

THIRD WOMAN.

How?   Where?

FIRST WOMAN.
> In the ashes of the bowl.

SECOND WOMAN.

While you were holding it between your hands?

THIRD WOMAN.

Speak quickly!

FIRST WOMAN.
> I have seen Cuchulain's roof-tree

Leap into fire, and the walls split and blacken.

SECOND WOMAN.

Cuchulain has gone out to die.

THIRD WOMAN.
> O! O!

SECOND WOMAN.

Who could have thought that one so great as he
Should meet his end at this unnoted sword!

FIRST WOMAN.

Life drifts between a fool and a blind man
To the end, and nobody can know his end.

SECOND WOMAN.

Come, look upon the quenching of this great-
ness.

[*The other two go to the door, but they stop for
a moment upon the threshold and wail.*

FIRST WOMAN.

No crying out, for there'll be need of cries
And knocking at the breast when it's all
finished.

[*The* WOMEN *go out. There is a sound of clash-
ing swords from time to time during what
follows.*

[*Enter the* FOOL *dragging the* BLIND MAN.

FOOL.

You have eaten it, you have eaten it! You
have left me nothing but the bones.

[*He throws* BLIND MAN *down by big chair.*

BLIND MAN.

O, that I should have to endure such a plague! O, I ache all over! O, I am pulled to pieces! This is the way you pay me all the good I have done you!

FOOL.

You have eaten it! You have told me lies. I might have known you had eaten it when I saw your slow, sleepy walk. Lie there till the kings come. O, I will tell Conchubar and Cuchulain and all the kings about you!

BLIND MAN.

What would have happened to you but for me, and you without your wits? If I did not take care of you, what would you do for food and warmth?

FOOL.

You take care of me! You stay safe, and send me into every kind of danger. You sent me down the cliff for gulls' eggs while you warmed your blind eyes in the sun; and then you ate all that were good for food. You left me the eggs that were neither egg nor bird. [BLIND MAN *tries to rise;* FOOL *makes him lie down again.*] Keep quiet now, till I shut the door. There is

I

some noise outside—a high vexing noise, so
that I can't be listening to myself. [*Shuts the
big door.*] Why can't they be quiet! why can't
they be quiet! [BLIND MAN *tries to get away.*]
Ah! you would get away, would you! [*Follows*
BLIND MAN *and brings him back.*] Lie there! lie
there! No, you won't get away! Lie there till
the kings come. I'll tell them all about you.
I will tell it all. How you sit warming your-
self, when you have made me light a fire of
sticks, while I sit blowing it with my mouth.
Do you not always make me take the windy
side of the bush when it blows, and the rainy
side when it rains?

BLIND MAN.

Oh, good Fool! listen to me. Think of the
care I have taken of you. I have brought you
to many a warm hearth, where there was a
good welcome for you, but you would not stay
there; you were always wandering about.

FOOL.

The last time you brought me in it was not
I who wandered away, but you that got put
out because you took the crubeen out of the
pot when nobody was looking. Keep quiet,
now!

CUCHULAIN [*rushing in*].

Witchcraft! There is no witchcraft on the earth, or among the witches of the air, that these hands cannot break.

FOOL.

Listen to me, Cuchulain. I left him turning the fowl at the fire. He ate it all, though I had stolen it. He left me nothing but the feathers.

CUCHULAIN.

Fill me a horn of ale!

BLIND MAN.

I gave him what he likes best. You do not know how vain this fool is. He likes nothing so well as a feather.

FOOL.

He left me nothing but the bones and feathers. Nothing but the feathers, though I had stolen it.

CUCHULAIN.

Give me that horn! Quarrels here, too! [*Drinks.*] What is there between you two that is worth a quarrel? Out with it!

BLIND MAN.

Where would he be but for me? I must be always thinking—thinking to get food for the two of us, and when we've got it, if the moon is at the full or the tide on the turn, he'll leave the rabbit in the snare till it is full of maggots, or let the trout slip back through his hands into the stream.

[*The* FOOL *has begun singing while the* BLIND MAN *is speaking.*

FOOL [*singing*].

When you were an acorn on the tree-top,
　Then was I an eagle cock;
Now that you are a withered old block,
　Still am I an eagle cock.

BLIND MAN.

Listen to him, now.　That's the sort of talk I have to put up with day out, day in.

[*The* FOOL *is putting the feathers into his hair.* CUCHULAIN *takes a handful of feathers out of a heap the* FOOL *has on the bench beside him, and out of the* FOOL's *hair, and begins to wipe the blood from his sword with them.*

FOOL.

He has taken my feathers to wipe his sword. It is blood that he is wiping from his sword.

CUCHULAIN.

[*Goes up to door at back and throws away feathers.*]

They are standing about his body. They will not awaken him, for all his witchcraft.

BLIND MAN.

It is that young champion that he has killed. He that came out of Aoife's country.

CUCHULAIN.

He thought to have saved himself with witchcraft.

FOOL.

That blind man there said he would kill you. He came from Aoife's country to kill you. That blind man said they had taught him every kind of weapon that he might do it.   But I always knew that you would kill him.

CUCHULAIN [*to the* BLIND MAN].

You knew him, then?

BLIND MAN.

I saw him, when I had my eyes, in Aoife's country.

CUCHULAIN.

You were in Aoife's country?

BLIND MAN.

I knew him and his mother there.

CUCHULAIN.

He was about to speak of her when he died.

BLIND MAN.

He was a queen's son.

CUCHULAIN.

What queen? what queen? [*Seizes* BLIND MAN, *who is now sitting upon the bench.*] Was it Scathach? There were many queens. All the rulers there were queens.

BLIND MAN.

No, not Scathach.

CUCHULAIN.

It was Uathach, then? Speak! speak!

BLIND MAN.

I cannot speak; you are clutching me too tightly. [CUCHULAIN *lets him go.*] I cannot remember who it was. I am not certain. It was some queen.

FOOL.

He said a while ago that the young man was Aoife's son.

CUCHULAIN.

She? No, no! She had no son when I was there.

FOOL.

That blind man there said that she owned him for her son.

CUCHULAIN.

I had rather he had been some other woman's son. What father had he? A soldier out of Alba? She was an amorous woman—a proud, pale, amorous woman.

BLIND MAN.

None knew whose son he was.

CUCHULAIN.

None knew! Did you know, old listener at doors?

BLIND MAN.

No, no; I knew nothing.

FOOL.

He said awhile ago that he heard Aoife boast that she'd never but the one lover, and he the only man that had overcome her in battle.

[*Pause.*

BLIND MAN.

Somebody is trembling, Fool! The bench is
shaking. Why are you trembling? Is Cuchu-
lain going to hurt us? It was not I who told
you, Cuchulain.

FOOL.

It is Cuchulain who is trembling. It is
Cuchulain who is shaking the bench.

BLIND MAN.

It is his own son he has slain.

CUCHULAIN.

'Twas they that did it, the pale, windy people.
Where? where? where? My sword against
    the thunder!
But no, for they have always been my friends;
And though they love to blow a smoking coal
Till it's all flame, the wars they blow aflame
Are full of glory, and heart-uplifting pride,
And not like this. The wars they love awaken
Old fingers and the sleepy strings of harps.
Who did it, then? Are you afraid? Speak out!
For I have put you under my protection,
And will reward you well. Dubthach the
    Chafer?

He'd an old grudge.   No, for he is with Maeve.
Laegaire did it !   Why do you not speak?
What is this house? [*Pause.*] Now I remem-
  ber all.

> [*Comes before* CONCHUBAR's *chair, and strikes
> out with his sword, as if* CONCHUBAR *was
> sitting upon it.*

'Twas you who did it—you who sat up there
With your old rod of kingship, like a magpie
Nursing a stolen spoon.   No, not a magpie,
A maggot that is eating up the earth !
Yes, but a magpie, for he's flown away.
Where did he fly to ?

BLIND MAN.

He is outside the door.

CUCHULAIN.

Outside the door?

BLIND MAN.

Between the door and the sea.

CUCHULAIN.

Conchubar, Conchubar ! the sword into your
heart !

[*He rushes out. Pause.* FOOL *creeps up to the big door and looks after him.*

FOOL.

He is going up to King Conchubar. They are all about the young man. No, no, he is standing still. There is a great wave going to break, and he is looking at it. Ah! now he is running down to the sea, but he is holding up his sword as if he were going into a fight. [*Pause.*] Well struck! well struck!

BLIND MAN.

What is he doing now?

FOOL.

O! he is fighting the waves!

BLIND MAN.

He sees King Conchubar's crown on every one of them.

FOOL.

There, he has struck at a big one! He has struck the crown off it; he has made the foam fly. There again, another big one!

BLIND MAN.

Where are the kings? What are the kings doing?

FOOL.

They are shouting and running down to the shore, and the people are running out of the houses. They are all running.

BLIND MAN.

You say they are running out of the houses? There will be nobody left in the houses. Listen, Fool!

FOOL.

There, he is down! He is up again. He is going out into the deep water. There is a big wave. It has gone over him. I cannot see him now. He has killed kings and giants, but the waves have mastered him, the waves have mastered him!

BLIND MAN.

Come here, Fool!

FOOL.

The waves have mastered him.

BLIND MAN.

Come here!

FOOL.

The waves have mastered him.

BLIND MAN.

Come here, I say!

FOOL.

[*Coming towards him, but looking backward
towards the door.*]

What is it?

BLIND MAN.

There will be nobody in the houses. Come
this way; come quickly! The ovens will be
full. We will put our hands into the ovens.
[*They go out.*

DEIRDRE

PERSONS IN THE PLAY

Musicians

Fergus, *an old man*

Naisi, *a young king*

Deirdre, *his queen*

A dark-faced Messenger

Conchubar, *the old King of Uladh, who is still strong and vigorous*

Dark-faced Executioner

DEIRDRE

*A Guest-house in a wood. It is a rough house of
timber; through the doors and some of the windows
one can see the great spaces of the wood, the sky
dimming, night closing in. But a window to the
left shows the thick leaves of a coppice; the land-
scape suggests silence and loneliness. There is
a door to right and left, and through the side
windows one can see anybody who approaches
either door, a moment before he enters. In the
centre, a part of the house is curtained off; the
curtains are drawn. There are unlighted torches
in brackets on the walls. There is, at one side,
a small table with a chessboard and chessmen
upon it, and a wine flagon and loaf of bread.
At the other side of the room there is a brazier
with a fire; two women, with musical instruments
beside them, crouch about the brazier: they are
comely women of about forty. Another woman,
who carries a stringed instrument, enters hur-
riedly; she speaks, at first standing in the doorway.*

FIRST MUSICIAN.

I HAVE a story right, my wanderers,
That has so mixed with fable in our songs,

K

That all seemed fabulous. We are come, by
    chance,
Into King Conchubar's country, and this house
Is an old guest-house built for travellers
From the seashore to Conchubar's royal house,
And there are certain hills among these woods,
And there Queen Deirdre grew.

SECOND MUSICIAN.

              That famous queen
Who has been wandering with her lover, Naisi,
And none to friend but lovers and wild hearts?

FIRST MUSICIAN.

[*Going nearer to the brazier.*]

Some dozen years ago, King Conchubar found
A house upon a hillside in this wood,
And there a comely child with an old witch
To nurse her, and there's nobody can say
If she were human, or of those begot
By an invisible king of the air in a storm
On a king's daughter, or anything at all
Of who she was or why she was hidden there
But that she'd too much beauty for good luck.
He went up thither daily, till at last
She put on womanhood, and he lost peace,
And Deirdre's tale began. The King was old.

A month or so before the marriage day,
A young man, in the laughing scorn of his
    youth,
Naisi, the son of Usnach, climbed up there,
And having wooed, or, as some say, been wooed,
Carried her off.

SECOND MUSICIAN.

        The tale were well enough
Had it a finish.

FIRST MUSICIAN.

        Hush ! I have more to tell ;
But gather close that I may whisper it :
I speak of terrible, mysterious ends—
The secrets of a king.

SECOND MUSICIAN.

        There's none to hear !

FIRST MUSICIAN.

I have been to Conchubar's house, and followed up
A crowd of servants going out and in
With loads upon their heads : embroideries
To hang upon the walls, or new-mown rushes
To strew upon the floors, and came at length
To a great room.

SECOND MUSICIAN.

Be silent ; there are steps !

[*Enter* FERGUS, *an old man, who moves about from door to window excitedly through what follows.*

FERGUS.

You are musicians by these instruments,
And if as seems—for you are comely women—
You can praise love, you'll have the best of luck,
For there'll be two, before the night is in,
That bargained for their love, and paid for it
All that men value.   You have but the time
To weigh a happy music with the sad;
To find what is most pleasing to a lover,
Before the son of Usnach and his queen
Have passed this threshold.

FIRST MUSICIAN.

Deirdre and her man !

FERGUS.

I thought to find a message from the king,
And ran to meet it.   Is there no messenger
From Conchubar to Fergus, son of Rogh ?
I was to have found a message in this house.

FIRST MUSICIAN.

Are Deirdre and her lover tired of life ?

FERGUS.

You are not of this country, or you'd know
That they are in my charge, and all forgiven.

FIRST MUSICIAN.

We have no country but the roads of the world.

FERGUS.

Then you should know that all things change
   in the world,
And hatred turns to love and love to hate,
And even kings forgive.

FIRST MUSICIAN.

              An old man's love
Who casts no second line, is hard to cure;
His jealousy is like his love.

FERGUS.

             And that's but true.
You have learned something in your wanderings.
He was so hard to cure, that the whole court,
But I alone, thought it impossible;
Yet after I had urged it at all seasons,
I had my way, and all's forgiven now;
And you shall speak the welcome and the joy
That I lack tongue for.

FIRST MUSICIAN.

> Yet old men are jealous.

FERGUS [*going to door*].

I am Conchubar's near friend, and that weighed
    somewhat,
And it was policy to pardon them.
The need of some young, famous, popular man
To lead the troops, the murmur of the crowd,
And his own natural impulse, urged him to it.
They have been wandering half-a-dozen years.

FIRST MUSICIAN.

And yet old men are jealous.

FERGUS [*coming from door*].

> Sing the more sweetly

Because, though age is arid as a bone,
This man has flowered. I've need of music, too;
If this gray head would suffer no reproach,
I'd dance and sing—and dance till the hour
    ran out,
Because I have accomplished this good deed.

FIRST MUSICIAN.

Look there—there at the window, those dark
    men,

With murderous and outlandish-looking arms—
They've been about the house all day.

[*Dark-faced* MEN *with strange barbaric dress
and arms pass by the doors and windows.
They pass one by one and in silence.*

FERGUS [*looking after them*].

What are you?
Where do you come from, who is it sent you
   here?

FIRST MUSICIAN.

They will not answer you.

FERGUS.

They do not hear.

FIRST MUSICIAN.

Forgive my open speech, but to these eyes
That have seen many lands, they are such men
As kings will gather for a murderous task,
That neither bribes, commands, nor promises
Can bring their people to.

FERGUS.

And that is why
You harped upon an old man's jealousy.

A trifle sets you quaking. Conchubar's fame
Brings merchandise on every wind that blows.
They may have brought him Libyan dragon-
    skin,
Or the ivory of the fierce unicorn.

FIRST MUSICIAN.

If these be merchants, I have seen the goods
They have brought to Conchubar, and understood
His murderous purpose.

FERGUS.

                    Murderous, you say?
Why, what new gossip of the roads is this?
But I'll not hear.

FIRST MUSICIAN.

            It may be life or death.
There is a room in Conchubar's house, and there—

FERGUS.

Be silent, or I'll drive you from the door.
There's many a one that would do more than that,
And make it prison, or death, or banishment
To slander the High King.

        [Suddenly restraining himself and speaking
            gently.

                        He is my friend;
I have his oath, and I am well content.
I have known his mind as if it were my own
These many years, and there is none alive
Shall buzz against him, and I there to stop it.
I know myself, and him, and your wild thought
Fed on extravagant poetry, and lit
By such a dazzle of old fabulous tales
That common things are lost, and all that's
      strange
Is true because 'twere pity if it were not.
                  [*Going to the door again.*

Quick! quick! your instruments! they are
      coming now.
I hear the hoofs a-clatter.   Begin that song;
But what is it to be?   I'd have them hear
A music foaming up out of the house
Like wine out of a cup.   Come now, a verse
Of some old time not worth remembering,
And all the lovelier because a bubble.
Begin, begin, of some old king and queen,
Of Lugaidh Redstripe or another; no, not him,
He and his lady perished wretchedly.

            FIRST MUSICIAN [*singing*].

   'Why is it,' Queen Edain said,
      'If I do but climb the stair . . . .''

FERGUS.

Ah! that is better. . . . They are alighted now.
Shake all your cockscombs, children; these are
    lovers.   [FERGUS *goes out.*

FIRST MUSICIAN.

'Why is it,' Queen Edain said,
   'If I do but climb the stair
To the tower overhead,
   When the winds are calling there,
Or the gannets calling out,
   In waste places of the sky,
There's so much to think about,
   That I cry, that I cry?'

SECOND MUSICIAN.

But her goodman answered her:
   'Love would be a thing of naught
Had not all his limbs a stir
   Born out of immoderate thought;
Were he anything by half,
   Were his measure running dry.
Lovers, if they may not laugh,
   Have to cry, have to cry.'

[DEIRDRE, NAISI, *and* FERGUS *have been seen for
a moment through the windows, but now they
have entered.* NAISI *lays down shield and*

spear and helmet, as if weary. He goes to
the door opposite to the door he entered by.
He looks out on to the road that leads to CON-
CHUBAR'S *house. If he is anxious, he would*
not have FERGUS *or* DEIRDRE *notice it. Pre-*
sently he comes from the door, and goes to the
table where the chessboard is.

THE THREE MUSICIANS [*together*].
But is Edain worth a song
   Now the hunt begins anew?
Praise the beautiful and strong;
   Praise the redness of the yew;
Praise the blossoming apple-stem.
   But our silence had been wise.
What is all our praise to them,
   That have one another's eyes?

FERGUS.
You are welcome, lady.

DEIRDRE.
         Conchubar has not come.
Were the peace honest, he'd have come himself
To prove it so.

FERGUS.
    Being no more in love,

He stays in his own house, arranging where
The curlew and the plover go, and where
The speckled heath-cock in a golden dish.

DEIRDRE.

But there's no messenger.

FERGUS.

                 He'll come himself
When all's in readiness and night closed in;
But till that hour, these birds out of the waste
Shall put his heart and mind into the music.
There's many a day that I have almost wept
To think that one so delicately made
Might never know the sweet and natural life
Of women born to that magnificence,
Quiet and music, courtesy and peace.

DEIRDRE.

I have found life obscure and violent,
And think it ever so; but none the less
I thank you for your kindness, and thank these
That put it into music.

FERGUS.

             Your house has been
The hole of the badger or the den of the fox;
But all that's finished, and your days will pass

From this day out where life is smooth on the
    tongue,
Because the grapes were trodden long ago.

NAISI.

If I was childish, and had faith in omens,
I'd rather not have lit on that old chessboard
At my home-coming.

FERGUS.

        There's a tale about it—
It has been lying there these many years—
Some wild old sorrowful tale.

NAISI.

        It is the board
Where Lugaidh Redstripe and that wife of his,
Who had a seamew's body half the year,
Played at the chess upon the night they died.

FERGUS.

I can remember now a tale of treachery,
A broken promise and a journey's end;
But it were best forgot.

NAISI.

        If the tale is true,
When it was plain that they had been betrayed,

They moved the men, and waited for the end,
As it were bedtime, and had so quiet minds
They hardly winked their eyes when the sword
    flashed.

FERGUS.

She never could have played so, being a woman,
If she had not the cold sea's blood in her.

DEIRDRE.

I have heard that th' ever-living warn mankind
By changing clouds, and casual accidents,
Or what seem so.

FERGUS.

          If there had been ill luck
In lighting on this chessboard of a sudden,
This flagon that stood on it when we came
Has made all right again, for it should mean
All wrongs forgiven, hospitality
For bitter memory, peace after war,
While that loaf there should add prosperity.
Deirdre will see the world, as it were, new-made,
If she'll but eat and drink.

NAISI.

          The flagon's dry,
Full of old cobwebs, and the bread is mouldy,

Left by some traveller gone upon his way
These many weeks.

DEIRDRE.

No one to welcome us,
And a bare house upon the journey's end.
Is that the welcome that a king spreads out
For those that he would honour?

NAISI.

Hush! no more.
You are King Conchubar's guest, being in his
house.
You speak as women do that sit alone,
Marking the ashes with a stick till they
Are in a dreamy terror. Being a queen,
You should have too calm thought to start at
shadows.

FERGUS.

Come, let us look if there's a messenger
From Conchubar's house. A little way without
One sees the road for half a mile or so,
Where the trees thin or thicken.

NAISI.

When those we love
Speak words unfitting to the ear of kings,
Kind ears are deaf.

FERGUS.

Before you came
I had to threaten these that would have weighed
Some crazy phantasy of their own brain
Or gossip of the road with Conchubar's word.
If I had thought so little of mankind
I never could have moved him to this pardon.
I have believed the best of every man,
And find that to believe it is enough
To make a bad man show him at his best,
Or even a good man swing his lantern higher.

[NAISI *and* FERGUS *go out. The last words are
spoken as they go through the door. One can
see them through part of what follows, either
through door or window. They move about,
talking or looking along the road towards*
CONCHUBAR'S *house.*

FIRST MUSICIAN.

If anything lies heavy on your heart,
Speak freely of it, knowing it is certain
That you will never see my face again.

DEIRDRE.

You've been in love?

FIRST MUSICIAN.

If you would speak of love,

Speak freely. There is nothing in the world
That has been friendly to us but the kisses
That were upon our lips, and when we are old
Their memory will be all the life we have.

DEIRDRE.

There was a man that loved me. He was old;
I could not love him. Now I can but fear.
He has made promises, and brought me home;
But though I turn it over in my thoughts,
I cannot tell if they are sound and wholesome,
Or hackles on the hook.

FIRST MUSICIAN.

               I have heard he loved you,
As some old miser loves the dragon-stone
He hides among the cobwebs near the roof.

DEIRDRE.

You mean that when a man who has loved like
    that
Is after crossed, love drowns in its own flood,
And that love drowned and floating is but hate.
And that a king who hates, sleeps ill at night,
Till he has killed, and that, though the day
    laughs,
We shall be dead at cockcrow.

L

FIRST MUSICIAN.

You have not my thought.
When I lost one I loved distractedly,
I blamed my crafty rival and not him,
And fancied, till my passion had run out,
That could I carry him away with me,
And tell him all my love, I'd keep him yet.

DEIRDRE.

Ah! now I catch your meaning, that this
    king
Will murder Naisi, and keep me alive.

FIRST MUSICIAN.

'Tis you that put that meaning upon words
Spoken at random.

DEIRDRE.

Wanderers like you,
Who have their wit alone to keep their lives,
Speak nothing that is bitter to the ear
At random; if they hint at it at all
Their eyes and ears have gathered it so lately
That it is crying out in them for speech.

FIRST MUSICIAN.

We have little that is certain.

DEIRDRE.

Certain or not,
Speak it out quickly, I beseech you to it;
I never have met any of your kind,
But that I gave them money, food, and fire.

FIRST MUSICIAN.

There are strange, miracle-working, wicked
    stones,
Men tear out of the heart and the hot brain
Of Libyan dragons.

DEIRDRE.

The hot Istain stone,
And the cold stone of Fanes, that have power
To stir even those at enmity to love.

FIRST MUSICIAN.

They have so great an influence, if but sewn
In the embroideries that curtain in
The bridal bed.

DEIRDRE.

O Mover of the stars
That made this delicate house of ivory,
And made my soul its mistress, keep it safe.

FIRST MUSICIAN.

I have seen a bridal bed, so curtained in,

So decked for miracle in Conchubar's house,
And learned that a bride's coming.

DEIRDRE.

                              And I the bride?
Here is worse treachery than the seamew
        suffered,
For she but died and mixed into the dust
Of her dear comrade, but I am to live
And lie in the one bed with him I hate.
Where is Naisi? I was not alone like this
When Conchubar first chose me for his wife;
I cried in sleeping or waking and he came,
But now there is worse need.

NAISI [*entering with* FERGUS].

                              Why have you called?
I was but standing there, without the door.

DEIRDRE [*going to the other door*].

The horses are still saddled, follow me,
And hurry to our ships, and get us gone.

NAISI.

[*Stopping her and partly speaking to her,
        partly to* FERGUS.]

There's naught to fear; the king's forgiven all.
She has the heart of a wild bird that fears

The net of the fowler or the wicker cage,
And has been ever so. Although it's hard,
It is but needful that I stand against you,
And if I did not you'd despise me for it,
As women do the husbands that they lead
Whether for good or evil.

DEIRDRE.

               I have heard
Monstrous, terrible, mysterious things,
Magical horrors and the spells of wizards.

FERGUS.

Why, that's no wonder, you've been listening
To singers of the roads that gather up
The tales of the whole world, and when they
     weary
Imagine new, or lies about the living,
Because their brains are ever upon fire.

DEIRDRE.

Is then the king that sends no messenger,
And leaves an empty house before a guest,
So clear in all he does that no dim word
Can light us to a doubt?

FERGUS.

          However dim,
Speak it, for I have known King Conchubar

Better than my own heart, and I can quench
Whatever words have made you doubt him.

NAISI.

No,
I cannot weigh the gossip of the roads
With a king's word, and were the end but death,
I may not doubt him.

DEIRDRE.

Naisi, I must speak.

FERGUS.

Let us begone, this house is no fit place,
Being full of doubt—Deirdre is right.

> [*To* DEIRDRE, *who has gone towards the*
> *door she had entered by.*

No, no,
Not by that door that opens on the path
That runs to the seashore, but this that leads
To Conchubar's house. We'll wait no messenger,
But go to his well-lighted house, and there
Where the rich world runs up into a wick
And that burns steadily, because no wind
Can blow upon it, bring all doubts to an end.
The table has been spread by this, the court
Has ridden from all sides to welcome you
To safety and to peace.

DEIRDRE.

Safety and peace!
I had them when a child, but never since.

FERGUS.

Men blame you that you have stirred a quarrel up
That has brought death to many. I have poured
Water upon the fire, but if you fly
A second time the house is in a blaze
And all the screaming household can but blame
The savage heart of beauty for it all;
And Naisi that but helped to tar the wisp
Be but a hunted outlaw all his days.

DEIRDRE.

I will be blamed no more! there's but one way.
I'll spoil this beauty that brought misery
And houseless wandering on the man I loved,
And so buy peace between him and the king.
These wanderers will show me how to do it,
To clip my hair to baldness, blacken my skin
With walnut juice, and tear my face with briars.
Oh! that wild creatures of the woods had torn
This body with their claws.

NAISI.

What is your meaning?
What are you saying? That he loves you still?

DEIRDRE.

Whatever were to happen to this face,
I'd be myself; and there's not any way
But this way to bring trouble to an end.

NAISI.

Answer me—does King Conchubar still love—
Does he still covet you?

DEIRDRE.

        Tell out the plot,
The plan, the network, all the treachery,
And of the bridal chamber and the bed,
The magical stones, the wizard's handiwork.

NAISI.

Take care of Deirdre, if I die in this,
For she must never fall into his hands,
Whatever the cost.

DEIRDRE.

        Where would you go to, Naisi?

NAISI.

I go to drag the truth from Conchubar,
Before his people, in the face of his army,
And if it be as black as you have made it,
To kill him there.

DEIRDRE.

You never would return;
I'd never look upon your face again.
Oh, keep him, Fergus; do not let him go,
But hold him from it. You are both wise and
kind.

NAISI.

When you were all but Conchubar's wife, I
took you;
He tried to kill me, and he would have done it
If I had been so near as I am now.
And now that you are mine, he has planned to
take you.
Should I be less than Conchubar, being a man?

[*Dark-faced* MESSENGER *comes into the
house, unnoticed.*

MESSENGER.

Supper is on the table; Conchubar
Is waiting for his guests.

FERGUS.

All's well, again!
All's well! all's well! You cried your doubts
so loud,
That I had almost doubted.

NAISI.

I would have killed him,
And he the while but busy in his house
For the more welcome.

DEIRDRE.

The message is not finished.

FERGUS.

Come quickly. Conchubar will laugh, that I—
Although I held out boldly in my speech—
That I, even I—

DEIRDRE.

Wait, wait!   He is not done.

FERGUS.

That am so great a friend, have doubted him.

MESSENGER.

Deirdre, and Fergus, son of Rogh, are sum-
moned;
But not the traitor that bore off the queen.
It is enough that the king pardon her,
And call her to his table and his bed.

NAISI.

So, then, it's treachery.

FERGUS.

I'll not believe it.

NAISI.

Tell Conchubar to meet me in some place
Where none can come between us but our
   swords.

MESSENGER.

I have done my message; I am Conchubar's
   man;
I take no message from a traitor's lips.

[*He goes.*

NAISI.

No, but you must; and I will have you swear
To carry it unbroken.

[*He follows* MESSENGER *out.*

FERGUS.

He has been suborned.
I know King Conchubar's mind as it were my
   own;
I'll learn the truth from him.

[*He is about to follow* NAISI, *but* DEIRDRE
   stops him.

DEIRDRE.

No, no, old man,
You thought the best, and the worst came of it;
We listened to the counsel of the wise,
And so turned fools. But ride and bring your
　　friends.
Go, and go quickly. Conchubar has not seen
　　me;
It may be that his passion is asleep,
And that we may escape.

FERGUS.

But I'll go first,
And follow up that Libyan heel, and send
Such words to Conchubar, that he may know
At how great peril he lays hands upon you.

[NAISI *enters.*]

NAISI.

The Libyan, knowing that a servant's life
Is safe from hands like mine, but turned and
　　mocked.

FERGUS.

I'll call my friends, and call the reaping-hooks,
And carry you in safety to the ships.
My name has still some power. I will protect,
Or, if that is impossible, revenge.

[*Goes out by other door.*

NAISI.

[*Who is calm, like a man who has passed beyond life.*]
The crib has fallen and the birds are in it;
There is not one of the great oaks about us
But shades a hundred men.

DEIRDRE.

Let's out and die,
Or break away, if the chance favour us.

NAISI.

They would but drag you from me, stained
    with blood.
Their barbarous weapons would but mar that
    beauty,
And I would have you die as a queen should—
In a death chamber.   You are in my charge.
We will wait here, and when they come upon
    us,
I'll hold them from the doors, and when that's
    over,
Give you a cleanly death with this grey edge.

DEIRDRE.

I will stay here; but you go out and fight.
Our way of life has brought no friends to us,
And if we do not buy them leaving it,
We shall be ever friendless.

NAISI.

What do they say?
That Lugaidh Redstripe and that wife of his
Sat at this chessboard, waiting for their end.
They knew that there was nothing that could
          save them,
And so played chess as they had any night
For years, and waited for the stroke of sword.
I never heard a death so out of reach
Of common hearts, a high and comely end:
What need have I, that gave up all for love,
To die like an old king out of a fable,
Fighting and passionate? What need is there
For all that ostentation at my setting?
I have loved truly and betrayed no man.
I need no lightning at the end, no beating
In a vain fury at the cage's door.

[*To* MUSICIANS.]

Had you been here when that man and his
          queen
Played at so high a game, could you have found
An ancient poem for the praise of it?
It should have set out plainly that those two,
Because no man and woman have loved better,
Might sit on there contentedly, and weigh
The joy comes after. I have heard the seamew
Sat there, with all the colour in her cheeks,

As though she'd say: 'There's nothing happen-
      ing
But that a king and queen are playing chess.'

DEIRDRE.

He's in the right, though I have not been born
Of the cold, haughty waves. My veins are hot.
But though I have loved better than that queen,
I'll have as quiet fingers on the board.
Oh, singing women, set it down in a book
That love is all we need, even though it is
But the last drops we gather up like this;
And though the drops are all we have known of
      life,
For we have been most friendless—praise us for it
And praise the double sunset, for naught's
      lacking,
But a good end to the long, cloudy day.

NAISI.

Light torches there and drive the shadows out,
For day's red end comes up.

> [*A* MUSICIAN *lights a torch in the fire and then
> crosses before the chess-players, and slowly
> lights the torches in the sconces. The light is
> almost gone from the wood, but there is a clear
> evening light in the sky, increasing the sense
> of solitude and loneliness.*

DEIRDRE.

                    Make no sad music.
What is it but a king and queen at chess?
They need a music that can mix itself
Into imagination, but not break
The steady thinking that the hard game needs.

[*During the chess, the* MUSICIANS *sing this song.*]

        Love is an immoderate thing
            And can never be content,
        Till it dip an ageing wing,
            Where some laughing element
        Leaps and Time's old lanthorn dims.
            What's the merit in love-play,
        In the tumult of the limbs
            That dies out before 'tis day,
        Heart on heart, or mouth on mouth,
            All that mingling of our breath,
        When love-longing is but drouth
            For the things come after death?

[*During the last verses* DEIRDRE *rises from the
    board and kneels at* NAISI's *feet.*]

DEIRDRE.

I cannot go on playing like that woman
That had but the cold blood of the sea in her
    veins.

NAISI.

It is your move.   Take up your man again.

DEIRDRE.

Do you remember that first night in the woods
We lay all night on leaves, and looking up,
When the first grey of the dawn awoke the birds,
Saw leaves above us.   You thought that I still
    slept,
And bending down to kiss me on the eyes,
Found they were open.   Bend and kiss me now,
For it may be the last before our death.
And when that's over, we'll be different;
Imperishable things, a cloud or a fire.
And I know nothing but this body, nothing
But that old vehement, bewildering kiss.

[CONCHUBAR *comes to the door.*]

MUSICIAN.

Children, beware!

NAISI [*laughing*].

            He has taken up my challenge;
Whether I am a ghost or living man
When day has broken, I'll forget the rest,
And say that there is kingly stuff in him.

   [*Turns to fetch spear and shield, and then sees
    that* CONCHUBAR *has gone.*

                                    M

DEIRDRE.

He came to spy upon us, not to fight.

NAISI.

A prudent hunter, therefore, but no king.
He'd find if what has fallen in the pit
Were worth the hunting, but has come too
　　　near,
And I turn hunter. You're not man, but beast.
Go scurry in the bushes, now, beast, beast,
For now it's topsy-turvy, I upon you.

　　　　　[*He rushes out after* CONCHUBAR.

DEIRDRE.

You have a knife there thrust into your girdle.
I'd have you give it me.

MUSICIAN.

　　　　　No, but I dare not.

DEIRDRE.

No, but you must.

MUSICIAN.

　　　　　If harm should come to you,
They'd know I gave it.

　　　DEIRDRE [*snatching knife*].

　　　　　There is no mark on this

To make it different from any other
Out of a common forge.

> [*Goes to the door and looks out.*

MUSICIAN.

You have taken it,
I did not give it you; but there are times
When such a thing is all the friend one has.

DEIRDRE.

The leaves hide all, and there's no way to find
What path to follow. Why is there no sound?

> [*She goes from door to window.*

MUSICIAN.

Where would you go?

DEIRDRE.

To strike a blow for Naisi,
If Conchubar call the Libyans to his aid.
But why is there no clash? They have met
by this!

MUSICIAN.

Listen. I am called far-seeing. If Conchubar win,
You have a woman's wile that can do much,
Even with men in pride of victory.
He is in love and old. What were one knife
Among a hundred?

DEIRDRE [*going towards them*].
                Women, if I die,
If Naisi die this night, how will you praise?
What words seek out? for that will stand to
        you;
For being but dead we shall have many friends.
All through your wanderings, the doors of
        kings
Shall be thrown wider open, the poor man's
        hearth
Heaped with new turf, because you are wearing
        this   [*Gives* MUSICIAN *a bracelet.*
To show that you have Deirdre's story right.

MUSICIAN.

Have you not been paid servants in love's house
To sweep the ashes out and keep the doors?
And though you have suffered all for mere
        love's sake
You'd live your lives again.

DEIRDRE.

                Even this last hour.

[CONCHUBAR *enters with dark-faced men.*]

CONCHUBAR.

One woman and two men; that is a quarrel

That knows no mending.   Bring the man she
    chose
Because of his beauty and the strength of his
    youth.

   [*The dark-faced men drag in* NAISI *entangled
    in a net.*

NAISI.

I have been taken like a bird or a fish.

CONCHUBAR.

He cried 'Beast, beast!' and in a blind-beast rage
He ran at me and fell into the nets,
But we were careful for your sake, and took
    him
With all the comeliness that woke desire
Unbroken in him.   I being old and lenient—
I would not hurt a hair upon his head.

DEIRDRE.

What do you say?   Have you forgiven him?

NAISI.

He is but mocking us.   What's left to say
Now that the seven years' hunt is at an end?

DEIRDRE.

He never doubted you until I made him,

And therefore all the blame for what he says
Should fall on me.

CONCHUBAR.

         But his young blood is hot,
And if we're of one mind, he shall go free,
And I ask nothing for it, or, if something,
Nothing I could not take.   There is no king
In the wide world that, being so greatly
      wronged,
Could copy me, and give all vengeance up.
Although her marriage-day had all but come,
You carried her away; but I'll show mercy.
Because you had the insolent strength of youth
You carried her away; but I've had time
To think it out through all these seven years.
I will show mercy.

NAISI.

You have many words.

CONCHUBAR.

I will not make a bargain; I but ask
What is already mine.   You may go free
If Deirdre will but walk into my house
Before the people's eyes, that they may know
When I have put the crown upon her head
I have not taken her by force and guile.

The doors are open, and the floors are strewed,
And in the bridal chamber curtains sewn
With all enchantments that give happiness,
By races that are germane to the sun,
And nearest him, and have no blood in their
    veins—
For when they're wounded the wound drips
    with wine—
Nor speech but singing. At the bridal door
Two fair king's daughters carry in their hands
The crown and robe.

DEIRDRE.

                    Oh, no! Not that, not that.
Ask any other thing but that one thing.
Leave me with Naisi. We will go away
Into some country at the ends of the earth.
We'll trouble you no more. You will be
    praised
By everybody if you pardon us.
'He is good, he is good,' they'll say to one
    another;
'There's nobody like him, for he forgave
Deirdre and Naisi.'

CONCHUBAR.

                    Do you think that I
Shall let you go again, after seven years

Of longing and of planning here and there,
And trafficking with merchants for the stones
That make all sure, and watching my own face
That none might read it?

DEIRDRE [*to* NAISI].

It's better to go with him.
Why should you die when one can bear it all?
My life is over; it's better to obey.
Why should you die? I will not live long, Naisi.
I'd not have you believe I'd long stay living;
Oh no, no, no! You will go far away.
You will forget me. Speak, speak, Naisi, speak,
And say that it is better that I go.
I will not ask it. Do not speak a word,
For I will take it all upon myself.
Conchubar, I will go.

NAISI.

And do you think
That, were I given life at such a price,
I would not cast it from me? O, my eagle!
Why do you beat vain wings upon the rock
When hollow night's above?

DEIRDRE.

It's better, Naisi.
It may be hard for you, but you'll forget.

For what am I, to be remembered always?
And there are other women. There was one,
The daughter of the King of Leodas;
I could not sleep because of her. Speak to him;
Tell it out plain, and make him understand.
And if it be he thinks I shall stay living,
Say that I will not.

NAISI.

Would I had lost life
Among those Scottish kings that sought it of me,
Because you were my wife, or that the worst
Had taken you before this bargaining!
O eagle! if you were to do this thing,
And buy my life of Conchubar with your body,
Love's law being broken, I would stand alone
Upon the eternal summits, and call out,
And you could never come there, being banished.

DEIRDRE [*kneeling to* CONCHUBAR].
I would obey, but cannot.   Pardon us.
I know that you are good.   I have heard you praised
For giving gifts; and you will pardon us,
Although I cannot go into your house.
It was my fault.   I only should be punished.

[*Unseen by* DEIRDRE, NAISI *is gagged.*

The very moment these eyes fell on him,
I told him; I held out my hands to him;
How could he refuse? At first he would not—
I am not lying—he remembered you.
What do I say? My hands?—No, no, my lips—
For I had pressed my lips upon his lips—
I swear it is not false—my breast to his;

    [CONCHUBAR *motions;* NAISI, *unseen by* DEIRDRE,
      is taken behind the curtain.

Until I woke the passion that's in all,
And how could he resist? I had my beauty.
You may have need of him, a brave, strong man,
Who is not foolish at the council board,
Nor does he quarrel by the candle-light
And give hard blows to dogs. A cup of wine
Moves him to mirth, not madness.

                    [*She stands up.*

               What am I saying?
You may have need of him, for you have none
Who is so good a sword, or so well loved
Among the common people. You may need
    him,
And what king knows when the hour of need
    may come?
You dream that you have men enough. You
    laugh.
Yes; you are laughing to yourself. You say,

'I am Conchubar—I have no need of him.'
You will cry out for him some day and say,
'If Naisi were but living'——[*She misses* NAISI.]
    Where is he?
Where have you sent him? Where is the son
    of Usna?
Where is he, O, where is he?

   [*She staggers over to the* MUSICIANS. *The*
   EXECUTIONER *has come out with sword on*
   which there is blood; CONCHUBAR *points to it.*
   The MUSICIANS *give a wail.*

CONCHUBAR.

The traitor who has carried off my wife
No longer lives. Come to my house now,
    Deirdre,
For he that called himself your husband's dead.

DEIRDRE.

O, do not touch me. Let me go to him.
                     [*Pause.*
King Conchubar is right. My husband's dead.
A single woman is of no account,
Lacking array of servants, linen cupboards,
The bacon hanging—and King Conchubar's
    house
All ready, too—I'll to King Conchubar's house.

It is but wisdom to do willingly
What has to be.

CONCHUBAR.

         But why are you so calm?
I thought that you would curse me and cry
     out,
And fall upon the ground and tear your hair.

DEIRDRE [*laughing*].

You know too much of women to think so;
Though, if I were less worthy of desire,
I would pretend as much; but, being myself,
It is enough that you were master here.
Although we are so delicately made,
There's something brutal in us, and we are won
By those who can shed blood. It was some
     woman
That taught you how to woo: but do not
     touch me,
For I'll go with you and do all your will
When I have done whatever's customary.
We lay the dead out, folding up the hands,
Closing the eyes, and stretching out the feet,
And push a pillow underneath the head,
Till all's in order; and all this I'll do
For Naisi, son of Usna.

CONCHUBAR.

It is not fitting.
You are not now a wanderer, but a queen,
And there are plenty that can do these things.

DEIRDRE.

[*Motioning* CONCHUBAR *away.*]
No, no.   Not yet.   I cannot be your queen
Till the past's finished, and its debts are paid.
When a man dies and there are debts unpaid,
He wanders by the debtor's bed and cries,
There's so much owing.

CONCHUBAR.

You are deceiving me.
You long to look upon his face again.
Why should I give you now to a dead man
That took you from a living?

[*He makes a step towards her.*

DEIRDRE.

In good time.
You'll stir me to more passion than he could,
And yet, if you are wise, you'll grant me this:
That I go look upon him that was once
So strong and comely and held his head so high
That women envied me.   For I will see him
All blood-bedabbled and his beauty gone.

It's better, when you're beside me in your
　　　strength,
That the mind's eye should call up the soiled
　　　body,
And not the shape I loved.　Look at him,
　　　women.
He heard me pleading to be given up,
Although my lover was still living, and yet
He doubts my purpose.　I will have you tell
　　　him
How changeable all women are.　How soon
Even the best of lovers is forgot,
When his day's finished.

CONCHUBAR.

　　　　　　No; but I will trust
The strength you have spoken of, and not
　　　your purpose.

DEIRDRE [*almost with a caress*].

I'll have this gift—the first that I have asked.
He has refused.　There is no sap in him,
Nothing but empty veins. I thought as much.
He has refused me the first thing I have asked—
Me, me, his wife.　I understand him now;
I know the sort of life I'll have with him;
But he must drag me to his house by force.

If he refuse [*she laughs*], he shall be mocked
    of all.
They'll say to one another, 'Look at him
That is so jealous that he lured a man
From over sea, and murdered him, and yet
He trembled at the thought of a dead face!'
        [She has her hand upon curtain.

CONCHUBAR.

How do I know that you have not some knife,
And go to die upon his body?

DEIRDRE.

              Have me searched,
If you would make so little of your queen.
It may be that I have a knife hid here
Under my dress. Bid one of these dark slaves
To search me for it.   *[Pause.*

CONCHUBAR.

      Go to your farewells, queen.

DEIRDRE.

Now strike the wire, and sing to it awhile,
Knowing that all is happy, and that you know
Within what bride-bed I shall lie this night,
And by what man, and lie close up to him,

For the bed's narrow, and there outsleep the
    cockcrow.   [*She goes behind the curtain.*

FIRST MUSICIAN.

They are gone, they are gone.   The proud
    may lie by the proud.

SECOND MUSICIAN.

Though we were bidden to sing, cry nothing
    loud.

FIRST MUSICIAN.

They are gone, they are gone.

SECOND MUSICIAN.

          Whispering were enough.

FIRST MUSICIAN.

Into the secret wilderness of their love.

SECOND MUSICIAN.

A high, grey cairn.   What more is to be said?

FIRST MUSICIAN.

Eagles have gone into their cloudy bed.

    [*Shouting outside.* FERGUS *enters. Many men
        with scythes and sickles and torches gather
        about the doors. The house is lit with the
        glare of their torches.*

FERGUS.

Where's Naisi, son of Usna, and his queen?
I and a thousand reaping-hooks and scythes
Demand him of you.

CONCHUBAR.

You have come too late.
I have accomplished all.   Deirdre is mine;
She is my queen, and no man now can rob me.
I had to climb the topmost bough and pull
This apple among the winds. Open the curtain,
That Fergus learn my triumph from her lips.
   [*The curtain is drawn back. The* MUSICIANS
       begin to keen with low voices.

No, no; I'll not believe it. She is not dead—
She cannot have escaped a second time!

FERGUS.

King, she is dead; but lay no hand upon her.
What's this but empty cage and tangled wire,
Now the bird's gone? but I'll not have you
       touch it.

CONCHUBAR.

You are all traitors, all against me—all.
And she has deceived me for a second time.
And every common man may keep his wife,
But not the King.

N

[*Loud shouting outside:* 'Death to Conchubar!'
'Where is Naisi?' etc. *The dark-skinned
men gather round* CONCHUBAR *and draw their
swords; but he motions them away.*

I have no need of weapons,
There's not a traitor that dare stop my way.
Howl, if you will; but I, being king, did right
In choosing her most fitting to be queen,
And letting no boy lover take the sway.

THE SHADOWY WATERS

To Lady Gregory

I walked among the seven woods of Coole,
Shan-walla, where a willow-bordered pond
Gathers the wild duck from the winter dawn;
Shady Kyle-dortha; sunnier Kyle-na-gno,
Where many hundred squirrels are as happy
As though they had been hidden by green boughs,
Where old age cannot find them; Pairc-na-lea,
Where hazel and ash and privet blind the paths;
Dim Pairc-na-carraig, where the wild bees fling
Their sudden fragrances on the green air;
Dim Pairc-na-tarav, where enchanted eyes
Have seen immortal, mild, proud shadows walk;
Dim Inchy wood, that hides badger and fox
And marten-cat, and borders that old wood
Wise Biddy Early called the wicked wood:
Seven odours, seven murmurs, seven woods.
I had not eyes like those enchanted eyes,
Yet dreamed that beings happier than men
Moved round me in the shadows, and at night
My dreams were cloven by voices and by fires;
And the images I have woven in this story
Of Forgael and Dectora and the empty waters
Moved round me in the voices and the fires,
And more I may not write of, for they that cleave
The waters of sleep can make a chattering tongue
Heavy like stone, their wisdom being half silence.

How shall I name you, immortal, mild, proud
    shadows?
I only know that all we know comes from you,
And that you come from Eden on flying feet.
Is. Eden far away, or do you hide
From human thought, as hares and mice and coneys
That run before the reaping-hook and lie
In the last ridge of the barley?   Do our woods
And winds and ponds cover more quiet woods,
More shining winds, more star-glimmering ponds?
Is Eden out of time and out of space?
And do you gather about us when pale light
Shining on water and fallen among leaves,
And winds blowing from flowers, and whirr of
    feathers
And the green quiet, have uplifted the heart?

I have made this poem for you, that men may read it
Before they read of Forgael and Dectora,
As men in the old times, before the harps began,
Poured out wine for the high invisible ones.

SEPTEMBER, 1900.

THE HARP OF AENGUS

Edain came out of Midher's hill, and lay
Beside young Aengus in his tower of glass,
Where time is drowned in odour-laden winds
And druid moons, and murmuring of boughs,
And sleepy boughs, and boughs where apples made
Of opal and ruby and pale chrysolite
Awake unsleeping fires; and wove seven strings,
Sweet with all music, out of his long hair,
Because her hands had been made wild by love;
When Midher's wife had changed her to a fly,
He made a harp with druid apple wood
That she among her winds might know he wept;
And from that hour he has watched over none
But faithful lovers.

THE SHADOWY WATERS

*The deck of an ancient ship.   At the right of the
stage is the mast, with a large square sail
hiding a great deal of the sky and sea on that
side.   The tiller is at the left of the stage; it is
a long oar coming through an opening in the
bulwark.   The deck rises in a series of steps
behind the tiller, and the stern of the ship curves
overhead.   All the woodwork is of dark green;
and the sail is dark green, with a blue pattern
upon it, having a little copper colour here and
there.   The sky and sea are dark blue.   All
the persons of the play are dressed in various
tints of green and blue, the men with helmets
and swords of copper, the woman with copper
ornaments upon her dress. When the play opens
there are four persons upon the deck.   AIBRIC
stands by the tiller.   FORGAEL sleeps upon the
raised portion of the deck towards the front of
the stage. Two SAILORS are standing near to the
mast, on which a harp is hanging.*

FIRST SAILOR.

HAS he not led us into these waste seas
For long enough?

SECOND SAILOR.

Aye, long and long enough.

FIRST SAILOR.

We have not come upon a shore or ship
These dozen weeks.

SECOND SAILOR.

And I had thought to make
A good round sum upon this cruise, and turn—
For I am getting on in life—to something
That has less ups and downs than robbery.

FIRST SAILOR.

I am so lecherous with abstinence
I'd give the profit of nine voyages
For that red Moll that had but the one eye.

SECOND SAILOR.

And all the ale ran out at the new moon;
And now that time puts water in my blood,
The ale cup is my father and my mother.

FIRST SAILOR.

It would be better to turn home again,
Whether he will or no; and better still
To make an end while he is sleeping there.
If we were of one mind I'd do it.

SECOND SAILOR.

                              Were't not
That there is magic in that harp of his,
That makes me fear to raise a hand against him,
I would be of your mind; but when he plays it
Strange creatures flutter up before one's eyes,
Or cry about one's ears.

FIRST SAILOR.

                    Nothing to fear.

SECOND SAILOR.

Do you remember when we sank that galley
At the full moon?

FIRST SAILOR.

              He played all through the night.

SECOND SAILOR.

Until the moon had set; and when I looked
Where the dead drifted, I could see a bird
Like a grey gull upon the breast of each.
While I was looking they rose hurriedly,
And after circling with strange cries awhile
Flew westward; and many a time since then
I've heard a rustling overhead in the wind.

FIRST SAILOR.

I saw them on that night as well as you.
But when I had eaten and drunk a bellyful
My courage came again.

SECOND SAILOR.

But that's not all.
The other night, while he was playing it,
A beautiful young man and girl came up
In a white, breaking wave; they had the look
Of those that are alive for ever and ever.

FIRST SAILOR.

I saw them, too, one night. Forgael was playing,
And they were listening there beyond the sail.
He could not see them, but I held out my hands
To grasp the woman.

SECOND SAILOR.

You have dared to touch her?

FIRST SAILOR.

O, she was but a shadow, and slipped from me.

SECOND SAILOR.

But were you not afraid?

FIRST SAILOR.

Why should I fear?

SECOND SAILOR.

'Twas Aengus and Edain, the wandering lovers,
To whom all lovers pray.

FIRST SAILOR.

But what of that?
A shadow does not carry sword or spear.

SECOND SAILOR.

My mother told me that there is not one
Of the ever-living half so dangerous
As that wild Aengus.   Long before her day
He carried Edain off from a king's house,
And hid her among fruits of jewel-stone
And in a tower of glass, and from that day
Has hated every man that's not in love,
And has been dangerous to him.

FIRST SAILOR.

I have heard
He does not hate seafarers as he hates
Peaceable men that shut the wind away,
And keep to the one weary marriage-bed.

SECOND SAILOR.

I think that he has Forgael in his net,
And drags him through the sea.

FIRST SAILOR.

                        Well, net or none,
I'd kill him while we have the chance to do it.

SECOND SAILOR.

It's certain I'd sleep easier o' nights
If he were dead; but who will be our captain,
Judge of the stars, and find a course for us?

FIRST SAILOR.

I've thought of that.   We must have Aibric
        with us,
For he can judge the stars as well as Forgael.
                [*Going towards* AIBRIC.
Become our captain, Aibric.   I am resolved
To make an end of Forgael while he sleeps.
There's not a man but will be glad of it
When it is over, nor one to grumble at us.
You'll have the captain's share of everything.

AIBRIC.

Silence! for you have taken Forgael's pay.

FIRST SAILOR.

We joined him for his pay, but have had none
This long while now; we had not turned against
        him

If he had brought us among peopled seas,
For that was in the bargain when we struck it.
What good is there in this hard way of living,
Unless we drain more flagons in a year
And kiss more lips than lasting peaceable men
In their long lives?   If you'll be of our troop
You'll be as good a leader.

AIBRIC.

     Be of your troop!
No, nor with a hundred men like you,
When Forgael's in the other scale.   I'd say it
Even if Forgael had not been my master
From earliest childhood, but that being so,
If you will draw that sword out of its scabbard
I'll give my answer.

FIRST SAILOR.

    You have awaked him.
      [*To* SECOND SAILOR.
We'd better go, for we have lost this chance.
       [*They go out.*

FORGAEL.

Have the birds passed us?   I could hear your
  voice.
But there were others.

AIBRIC.

I have seen nothing pass.

FORGAEL.

You're certain of it? I never wake from sleep
But that I am afraid they may have passed,
For they're my only pilots. If I lost them
Straying too far into the north or south,
I'd never come upon the happiness
That has been promised me. I have not seen them
These many days; and yet there must be many
Dying at every moment in the world,
And flying towards their peace.

AIBRIC.

Put by these thoughts,
And listen to me for awhile. The sailors
Are plotting for your death.

FORGAEL.

Have I not given
More riches than they ever hoped to find?
And now they will not follow, while I seek
The only riches that have hit my fancy.

AIBRIC.

What riches can you find in this waste sea
Where no ship sails, where nothing that's alive

Has ever come but those man-headed birds,
Knowing it for the world's end?

FORGAEL.

         Where the world ends
The mind is made unchanging, for it finds
Miracle, ecstasy, the impossible hope,
The flagstone under all, the fire of fires,
The roots of the world.

AIBRIC.

         Who knows that shadows
May not have driven you mad for their own
    sport?

FORGAEL.

Do you, too, doubt me? Have you joined their
    plot?

AIBRIC.

No, no, do not say that. You know right well
That I will never lift a hand against you.

FORGAEL.

Why should you be more faithful than the rest,
Being as doubtful?

AIBRIC.

         I have called you master
Too many years to lift a hand against you.

o

FORGAEL.

Maybe it is but natural to doubt me.
You've never known, I'd lay a wager on it,
A melancholy that a cup of wine,
A lucky battle, or a woman's kiss
Could not amend.

AIBRIC.

     I have good spirits enough.
I've nothing to complain of but heartburn,
And that is cured by a boiled liquorice root.

FORGAEL.

If you will give me all your mind awhile—
All, all, the very bottom of the bowl—
I'll show you that I am made differently,
That nothing can amend it but these waters,
Where I am rid of life—the events of the
  world—
What do you call it?—that old promise-breaker,
The cozening fortune-teller that comes whisper-
  ing,
'You will have all you have wished for when
  you have earned
Land for your children or money in a pot.'
And when we have it we are no happier,
Because of that old draught under the door,
Or creaky shoes. And at the end of all

We have been no better off than Seaghan the
    fool,
That never did a hand's turn. Aibric! Aibric!
We have fallen in the dreams the ever-living
Breathe on the burnished mirror of the world,
And then smooth out with ivory hands and
    sigh,
And find their laughter sweeter to the taste
For that brief sighing.

AIBRIC.

If you had loved some woman—

FORGAEL.

You say that also? You have heard the voices,
For that is what they say—all, all the shadows—
Aengus and Edain, those passionate wanderers,
And all the others; but it must be love
As they have known it. Now the secret's out;
For it is love that I am seeking for,
But of a beautiful, unheard-of kind
That is not in the world.

AIBRIC.

             And yet the world
Has beautiful women to please every man.

FORGAEL.

But he that gets their love after the fashion

Loves in brief longing and deceiving hope
And bodily tenderness, and finds that even
The bed of love, that in the imagination
Had seemed to be the giver of all peace,
Is no more than a wine-cup in the tasting,
And as soon finished.

AIBRIC.

All that ever loved.
Have loved that way—there is no other way.

FORGAEL.

Yet never have two lovers kissed but they
Believed there was some other near at hand,
And almost wept because they could not find it.

AIBRIC.

When they have twenty years; in middle life
They take a kiss for what a kiss is worth,
And let the dream go by.

FORGAEL.

It's not a dream,
But the reality that makes our passion
As a lamp shadow—no—no lamp, the sun.
What the world's million lips are thirsting for,
Must be substantial somewhere.

AIBRIC.

         I have heard the Druids
Mutter such things as they awake from trance.
It may be that the ever-living know it—
No mortal can.

FORGAEL.

        Yes; if they give us help.

AIBRIC.

They are besotting you as they besot
The crazy herdsman that will tell his fellows
That he has been all night upon the hills,
Riding to hurley, or in the battle-host
With the ever-living.

FORGAEL.

         What if he speak the truth,
And for a dozen hours have been a part
Of that more powerful life?

AIBRIC.

          His wife knows better.
Has she not seen him lying like a log,
Or fumbling in a dream about the house?
And if she hear him mutter of wild riders,
She knows that it was but the cart-horse
    coughing
That set him to the fancy.

FORGAEL.

                          All would be well
Could we but give us wholly to the dreams,
And get into their world that to the sense
Is shadow, and not linger wretchedly
Among substantial things; for it is dreams
That lift us to the flowing, changing world
That the heart longs for.   What is love itself,
Even though it be the lightest of light love,
But dreams that hurry from beyond the world
To make low laughter more than meat and drink,
Though it but set us sighing? Fellow-wanderer,
Could we but mix ourselves into a dream,
Not in its image on the mirror!

AIBRIC.

                          While
We're in the body that's impossible.

FORGAEL.

And yet I cannot think they're leading me
To death; for they that promised to me love
As those that can outlive the moon have
       known it,
Had the world's total life gathered up, it
       seemed,
Into their shining limbs—I've had great
       teachers.

Aengus and Edain ran up out of the wave—
You'd never doubt that it was life they promised
Had you looked on them face to face as I did,
With so red lips, and running on such feet,
And having such wide-open, shining eyes.

AIBRIC.

It's certain they are leading you to death.
None but the dead, or those that never lived,
Can know that ecstasy.   Forgael! Forgael!
They have made you follow the man-headed
        birds,
And you have told me that their journey lies
Towards the country of the dead.

FORGAEL.

                        What matter
If I am going to my death, for there,
Or somewhere, I shall find the love they have
        promised.
That much is certain.   I shall find a woman,
One of the ever-living, as I think—
One of the laughing people—and she and I
Shall light upon a place in the world's core,
Where passion grows to be a changeless thing,
Like charmed apples made of chrysoprase,
Or chrysoberyl, or beryl, or chrysolite;
And there, in juggleries of sight and sense,

Become one movement, energy, delight,
Until the overburthened moon is dead.
[*A number of* SAILORS *enter hurriedly.*]

FIRST SAILOR.

Look there! there in the mist! a ship of spice!
And we are almost on her!

SECOND SAILOR.

We had not known
But for the ambergris and sandalwood.

FIRST SAILOR.

No; but opoponax and cinnamon.

FORGAEL.

[*Taking the tiller from* AIBRIC.]
The ever-living have kept my bargain for me,
And paid you on the nail.

AIBRIC.

Take up that rope
To make her fast while we are plundering her.

FIRST SAILOR.

There is a king and queen upon her deck,
And where there is one woman there'll be
    others.

AIBRIC.

Speak lower, or they'll hear.

FIRST SAILOR.

They cannot hear;
They are too busy with each other.   Look!
He has stooped down and kissed her on the lips.

SECOND SAILOR.

When she finds out we have better men aboard
She may not be too sorry in the end.

FIRST SAILOR.

She will be like a wild cat; for these queens
Care more about the kegs of silver and gold,
And the high fame that come to them in
     marriage,
Than a strong body and a ready hand.

SECOND SAILOR.

There's nobody is natural but a robber,
And that is why the world totters about
Upon its bandy legs.

AIBRIC.

Run at them now,
And overpower the crew while yet asleep!
                    [*The* SAILORS *go out.*

[*Voices and the clashing of swords are heard from the other ship, which cannot be seen because of the sail.*]

A VOICE.

Armed men have come upon us! O, I am slain!

ANOTHER VOICE.

Wake all below!

ANOTHER VOICE.

Why have you broken our sleep?

FIRST VOICE.

Armed men have come upon us! O, I am slain!

FORGAEL.

[*Who has remained at the tiller.*]

There! there they come! Gull, gannet, or diver,
But with a man's head, or a fair woman's,
They hover over the masthead awhile
To wait their friends; but when their friends
    have come
They'll fly upon that secret way of theirs.
One—and one—a couple—five together;
And I will hear them talking in a minute.
Yes, voices! but I do not catch the words.

Now I can hear. There's one of them that says:
'How light we are, now we are changed to
    birds!'
Another answers: 'Maybe we shall find
Our heart's desire now that we are so light.'
And then one asks another how he died,
And says: 'A sword-blade pierced me in my
    sleep.'
And now they all wheel suddenly and fly
To the other side, and higher in the air.
And now a laggard with a woman's head
Comes crying, 'I have run upon the sword.
I have fled to my beloved in the air,
In the waste of the high air, that we may
    wander
Among the windy meadows of the dawn.'
But why are they still waiting? why are they
Circling and circling over the masthead?
What power that is more mighty than desire
To hurry to their hidden happiness
Withholds them now? Have the ever-living
    ones
A meaning in that circling overhead?
But what's the meaning? [*He cries out.*] Why
    do you linger there?
Why do you not run to your desire,
Now that you have happy winged bodies?
                    [*His voice sinks again.*

Being too busy in the air and the high air,
They cannot hear my voice; but what's the
    meaning?

[*The* SAILORS *have returned.* DECTORA *is with
    them. She is dressed in pale green, with copper
    ornaments on her dress, and has a copper crown
    upon her head. Her hair is dull red.*]

FORGAEL.

[*Turning and seeing her.*]

Why are you standing with your eyes upon me?
You are not the world's core. O no, no, no!
That cannot be the meaning of the birds.
You are not its core. My teeth are in the
    world,
But have not bitten yet.

DECTORA.

                    I am a queen,
And ask for satisfaction upon these
Who have slain my husband and laid hands
    upon me.

[*Breaking loose from the* SAILORS *who are hold-
    ing her.*]

Let go my hands!

FORGAEL.

Why do you cast a shadow?

Where do you come from? Who brought you
    to this place?
They would not send me one that casts a
    shadow.

DECTORA.

Would that the storm that overthrew my ships,
And drowned the treasures of nine conquered
    nations,
And blew me hither to my lasting sorrow,
Had drowned me also. But, being yet alive,
I ask a fitting punishment for all
That raised their hands against him.

FORGAEL.

                There are some
That weigh and measure all in these waste seas—
They that have all the wisdom that's in life,
And all that prophesying images
Made of dim gold rave out in secret tombs;
They have it that the plans of kings and queens
Are dust on the moth's wing; that nothing
    matters
But laughter and tears—laughter, laughter, and
    tears;
That every man should carry his own soul
Upon his shoulders.

DECTORA.

        You've nothing but wild words,

And I would know if you will give me ven-
	geance.

FORGAEL.

When she finds out I will not let her go—
When she knows that.

DECTORA.

	What is it that you are muttering—
That you'll not let me go?   I am a queen.

FORGAEL.

Although you are more beautiful than any,
I almost long that it were possible;
But if I were to put you on that ship,
With sailors that were sworn to do your will,
And you had spread a sail for home, a wind
Would rise of a sudden, or a wave so huge,
It had washed among the stars and put them
	out,
And beat the bulwark of your ship on mine,
Until you stood before me on the deck—
As now.

DECTORA.

	Does wandering in these desolate seas
And listening to the cry of wind and wave
Bring madness?

FORGAEL.

	Queen, I am not mad.

DECTORA.

And yet you say the water and the wind
Would rise against me.

FORGAEL.

　　　　No, I am not mad—
If it be not that hearing messages
From lasting watchers, that outlive the moon,
At the most quiet midnight is to be stricken.

DECTORA.

And did those watchers bid you take me cap-
　　tive?

FORGAEL.

Both you and I are taken in the net.
It was their hands that plucked the winds awake
And blew you hither; and their mouths have
　　promised
I shall have love in their immortal fashion.
They gave me that old harp of the nine spells
That is more mighty than the sun and moon,
Or than the shivering casting-net of the stars,
That none might take you from me.

DECTORA.

[*First trembling back from the mast where the
harp is, and then laughing.*]

　　　　　　For a moment
Your raving of a message and a harp

More mighty than the stars half troubled me.
But all that's raving. Who is there can compel
The daughter and granddaughter of kings
To be his bedfellow ?

FORGAEL.

Until your lips
Have called me their beloved, I'll not kiss them.

DECTORA.

My husband and my king died at my feet,
And yet you talk of love.

FORGAEL.

The movement of time
Is shaken in these seas, and what one does
One moment has no might upon the moment
That follows after.

DECTORA.

I understand you now.
You have a Druid craft of wicked sound
Wrung from the cold women of the sea—
A magic that can call a demon up,
Until my body give you kiss for kiss.

FORGAEL.

Your soul shall give the kiss.

DECTORA.

                              I am not afraid,
While there's a rope to run into a noose
Or wave to drown.   But I have done with
        words,
And I would have you look into my face
And know that it is fearless.

FORGAEL.

                              Do what you will,
For neither I nor you can break a mesh
Of the great golden net that is about us.

DECTORA.

There's nothing in the world that's worth a fear.

[She passes FORGAEL *and stands for a moment
        looking into his face.*

I have good reason for that thought.

*[She runs suddenly on to the raised part of the
        poop.*

                              And now
I can put fear away as a queen should.

[She mounts on to the bulwark and turns towards
        FORGAEL.

Fool, fool!   Although you have looked into
        my face
You do not see my purpose.   I shall have gone
Before a hand can touch me.

                                        P

FORGAEL [*folding his arms*].

My hands are still;
The ever-living hold us. Do what you will,
You cannot leap out of the golden net.

FIRST SAILOR.

No need to drown, for, if you will pardon us
And measure out a course and bring us home,
We'll put this man to death.

DECTORA.

I promise it.

FIRST SAILOR.

There is none to take his side.

AIBRIC.

I am on his side.
I'll strike a blow for him to give him time
To cast his dreams away.

[AIBRIC *goes in front of* FORGAEL *with drawn
sword.* FORGAEL *takes the harp.*

FIRST SAILOR.

No other'll do it.

[*The* SAILORS *throw* AIBRIC *on one side. He falls
upon the deck towards the poop. They lift their
swords to strike* FORGAEL, *who is about to play
the harp. The stage begins to darken. The*
SAILORS *hesitate in fear.*

SECOND SAILOR.

He has put a sudden darkness over the moon.

DECTORA.

Nine swords with handles of rhinoceros horn
To him that strikes him first!

FIRST SAILOR.

                       I will strike him first.

[*He goes close up to* FORGAEL *with his sword
    lifted. The harp begins to give out a faint
    light. The scene has become so dark that the
    only light is from the harp.*

[*Shrinking back.*] He has caught the crescent
    moon out of the sky,
And carries it between us.

SECOND SAILOR.

                      Holy fire
Has come into the jewels of the harp
To burn us to the marrow if we strike.

DECTORA.

I'll give a golden galley full of fruit,
That has the heady flavour of new wine,
To him that wounds him to the death.

FIRST SAILOR.

                        I'll do it.
For all his spells will vanish when he dies,
Having their life in him.

SECOND SAILOR.

Though it be the moon
That he is holding up between us there,
I will strike at him.

THE OTHERS.

And I! And I! And I!

[FORGAEL *plays the harp*.

FIRST SAILOR.

[*Falling into a dream suddenly*.]
But you were saying there is somebody
Upon that other ship we are to wake.
You did not know what brought him to his end,
But it was sudden.

SECOND SAILOR.

You are in the right;
I had forgotten that we must go wake him.

DECTORA.

He has flung a Druid spell upon the air,
And set you dreaming.

SECOND SAILOR.

How can we have a wake
When we have neither brown nor yellow ale?

FIRST SAILOR.

I saw a flagon of brown ale aboard her.

THIRD SAILOR.

How can we raise the keen that do not know
What name to call him by?

FIRST SAILOR.

                Come to his ship.
His name will come into our thoughts in a
    minute.
I know that he died a thousand years ago,
And has not yet been waked.

SECOND SAILOR [*beginning to keen*].
              Ohone! O! O! O!
The yew bough has been broken into two,
And all the birds are scattered.

ALL THE SAILORS.
              O! O! O! O!
            [*They go out keening.*

DECTORA.

Protect me now, gods, that my people swear by.

    [AIBRIC *has risen from the ground where he had
       fallen. He has begun looking for his sword
       as if in a dream.*

AIBRIC.

Where is my sword that fell out of my hand
When I first heard the news? Ah, there it is!

    [*He goes dreamily towards the sword, but* DEC-
       TORA *runs at it and takes it up before he can
       reach it.*

AIBRIC [*sleepily*].
Queen, give it me.

DECTORA.
No, I have need of it.

AIBRIC.
Why do you need a sword?   But you may
    keep it,
Now that he's dead I have no need of it,
For everything is gone.

A SAILOR.
[*Calling from the other ship.*]
                    Come hither, Aibric,
And tell me who it is that we are waking.

AIBRIC.
[*Half to* DECTORA, *half to himself.*]
What name had that dead king?   Arthur of
    Britain?
No, no—not Arthur.   I remember now.
It was golden-armed Iollan, and he died
Brokenhearted, having lost his queen
Through wicked spells.   That is not all the
    tale,
For he was killed.   O! O! O! O! O! O!
For golden-armed Iollan has been killed.
                    [*He goes out.*

[*While he has been speaking, and through part
of what follows, one hears the wailing of the
SAILORS from the other ship.* DECTORA *stands
with the sword lifted in front of* FORGAEL.

DECTORA.

I will end all your magic on the instant.

[*Her voice becomes dreamy, and she lowers the
sword slowly, and finally lets it fall. She
spreads out her hair. She takes off her crown
and lays it upon the deck.*

This sword is to lie beside him in the grave.
It was in all his battles. I will spread my hair,
And wring my hands, and wail him bitterly,
For I have heard that he was proud and laughing,
Blue-eyed, and a quick runner on bare feet,
And that he died a thousand years ago.
O ! O ! O !

                    [FORGAEL *changes the tune.*

        But no, that is not it.
I knew him well, and while I heard him laughing
They killed him at my feet. O ! O ! O ! O !
For golden-armed Iollan that I loved.
But what is it that made me say I loved him?
It was that harper put it in my thoughts,
But it is true. Why did they run upon him,
And beat the golden helmet with their swords?

FORGAEL.

Do you not know me, lady?   I am he
That you are weeping for.

DECTORA.

No, for he is dead.
O ! O ! O ! for golden-armed Iollan.

FORGAEL.

It was so given out, but I will prove
That the grave-diggers in a dreamy frenzy
Have buried nothing but my golden arms.
Listen to that low-laughing string of the moon
And you will recollect my face and voice,
For you have listened to me playing it
These thousand years.

[*He starts up, listening to the birds. The harp
slips from his hands, and remains leaning
against the bulwarks behind him. The light
goes out of it.*

What are the birds at there?
Why are they all a-flutter of a sudden?
What are you calling out above the mast?
If railing and reproach and mockery
Because I have awakened her to love
My magic strings, I'll make this answer to it:
Being driven on by voices and by dreams
That were clear messages from the ever-living,

I have done right.   What could I but obey?
And yet you make a clamour of reproach.

DECTORA [*laughing*].

Why, it's a wonder out of reckoning
That I should keen him from the full of the
    moon
To the horn, and he be hale and hearty.

FORGAEL.

How have I wronged her now that she is merry?
But no, no, no! your cry is not against me.
You know the councils of the ever-living,
And all that tossing of your wings is joy,
And all that murmuring 's but a marriage song;
But if it be reproach, I answer this:
There is not one among you that made love
By any other means.   You call it passion,
Consideration, generosity;
But it was all deceit, and flattery
To win a woman in her own despite,
For love is war, and there is hatred in it;
And if you say that she came willingly—

DECTORA.

Why do you turn away and hide your face,
That I would look upon for ever?

FORGAEL.

My grief.

DECTORA.

Have I not loved you for a thousand years?

FORGAEL.

I never have been golden-armed Iollan.

DECTORA.

I do not understand.   I know your face
Better than my own hands.

FORGAEL.

I have deceived you
Out of all reckoning.

DECTORA.

Is it not true
That you were born a thousand years ago,
In islands where the children of Aengus wind
In happy dances under a windy moon,
And that you'll bring me there?

FORGAEL.

I have deceived you;
I have deceived you utterly.

DECTORA.

How can that be?
Is it that though your eyes are full of love

Some other woman has a claim on you,
And I've but half?

FORGAEL.

Oh, no!

DECTORA.

And if there is,
If there be half a hundred more, what matter?
I'll never give another thought to it;
No, no, nor half a thought; but do not speak.
Women are hard and proud and stubborn-
hearted,
Their heads being turned with praise and
flattery;
And that is why their lovers are afraid
To tell them a plain story.

FORGAEL.

That's not the story;
But I have done so great a wrong against you,
There is no measure that it would not burst.
I will confess it all.

DECTORA.

What do I care,
Now that my body has begun to dream,
And you have grown to be a burning sod
In the imagination and intellect?

If something that's most fabulous were true—
If you had taken me by magic spells,
And killed a lover or husband at my feet—
I would not let you speak, for I would know
That it was yesterday and not to-day
I loved him; I would cover up my ears,
As I am doing now. [*A pause.*] Why do you
    weep?

FORGAEL.

I weep because I've nothing for your eyes
But desolate waters and a battered ship.

DECTORA.

O, why do you not lift your eyes to mine?

FORGAEL.

I weep—I weep because bare night's above,
And not a roof of ivory and gold.

DECTORA.

I would grow jealous of the ivory roof,
And strike the golden pillars with my hands.
I would that there was nothing in the world
But my beloved—that night and day had
    perished,
And all that is and all that is to be,
All that is not the meeting of our lips.

FORGAEL.

I too, I too.   Why do you look away?
Am I to fear the waves, or is the moon
My enemy?

DECTORA.

I looked upon the moon,
Longing to knead and pull it into shape
That I might lay it on your head as a crown.
But now it is your thoughts that wander away,
For you are looking at the sea.   Do you not
    know
How great a wrong it is to let one's thought
Wander a moment when one is in love?
  [*He has moved away. She follows him. He is
    looking out over the sea, shading his eyes.*]
Why are you looking at the sea?

FORGAEL.

             Look there!

DECTORA.

What is there but a troop of ash-grey birds
That fly into the west?

FORGAEL.

        But listen, listen!

DECTORA.

What is there but the crying of the birds?

FORGAEL.

If you'll but listen closely to that crying
You'll hear them calling out to one another
With human voices.

DECTORA.

O, I can hear them now.
What are they?   Unto what country do they
fly?

FORGAEL.

To unimaginable happiness.
They have been circling over our heads in the
air,
But now that they have taken to the road
We have to follow, for they are our pilots;
And though they're but the colour of grey ash,
They're crying out, could you but hear their
words,
'There is a country at the end of the world
Where no child's born but to outlive the moon.'

[*The* SAILORS *come in with* AIBRIC. *They are in
great excitement.*

FIRST SAILOR.

The hold is full of treasure.

SECOND SAILOR.

Full to the hatches.

FIRST SAILOR.
Treasure and treasure.

THIRD SAILOR.
Boxes of precious spice.

FIRST SAILOR.
Ivory images with amethyst eyes.

THIRD SAILOR.
Dragons with eyes of ruby.

FIRST SAILOR.
The whole ship
Flashes as if it were a net of herrings.

THIRD SAILOR.
Let's home; I'd give some rubies to a woman.

SECOND SAILOR.
There's somebody I'd give the amethyst eyes to.

FIRST SAILOR.
Let's home and spend it in our villages.

AIBRIC.
[*Silencing them with a gesture.*]
We would return to our own country, Forgael,
For we have found a treasure that's so great

Imagination cannot reckon it.
And having lit upon this woman there,
What more have you to look for on the seas?

FORGAEL.

I cannot—I am going on to the end.
As for this woman, I think she is coming with me.

AIBRIC.

The ever-living have made you mad; but no,
It was this woman in her woman's vengeance
That drove you to it, and I fool enough
To fancy that she'd bring you home again.
'Twas you that egged him to it, for you know
That he is being driven to his death.

DECTORA.

That is not true, for he has promised me
An unimaginable happiness.

AIBRIC.

And if that happiness be more than dreams,
More than the froth, the feather, the dustwhirl,
The crazy nothing that I think it is,
It shall be in the country of the dead,
If there be such a country.

DECTORA.

          No, not there,
But in some island where the life of the world

Leaps upward, as if all the streams o' the world
Had run into one fountain.

AIBRIC.

Speak to him.
He knows that he is taking you to death;
Speak—he will not deny it.

DECTORA.

Is that true?

FORGAEL.

I do not know for certain, but I know
That I have the best of pilots.

AIBRIC.

Shadows, illusions,
That the shape-changers, the ever-laughing
    ones,
The immortal mockers have cast into his mind,
Or called before his eyes.

DECTORA.

O carry me
To some sure country, some familiar place.
Have we not everything that life can give
In having one another?

Q

FORGAEL.

How could I rest
If I refused the messengers and pilots
With all those sights and all that crying out?

DECTORA.

But I will cover up your eyes and ears,
That you may never hear the cry of the birds,
Or look upon them.

FORGAEL.

Were they but lowlier
I'd do your will, but they are too high—too
    high.

DECTORA.

Being too high, their heady prophecies
But harry us with hopes that come to nothing,
Because we are not proud, imperishable,
Alone and winged.

FORGAEL.

Our love shall be like theirs
When we have put their changeless image on.

DECTORA.

I am a woman, I die at every breath.

AIBRIC.

Let the birds scatter for the tree is broken.
And there's no help in words. [*To the* SAILORS.]
   To the other ship,
And I will follow you and cut the rope
When I have said farewell to this man here,
For neither I nor any living man
Will look upon his face again.
          [*The* SAILORS *go out.*

FORGAEL [*to* DECTORA].

          Go with him,
For he will shelter you and bring you home.

AIBRIC.

[*Taking* FORGAEL'S *hand.*]
I'll do it for his sake.

DECTORA.

       No. Take this sword
And cut the rope, for I go on with Forgael.

AIBRIC.

[*Half-falling into the keen.*]
The yew bough has been broken into two,
And all the birds are scattered—O ! O ! O !
Farewell ! farewell !   [*He goes out.*

DECTORA.

                    The sword is in the rope—
The rope's in two—it falls into the sea,
It whirls into the foam.   O ancient worm,
Dragon that loved the world and held us to it,
You are broken, you are broken.   The world
        drifts away,
And I am left alone with my beloved,
Who cannot put me from his sight for ever.
We are alone for ever, and I laugh,
Forgael, because you cannot put me from you.
The mist has covered the heavens, and you and I
Shall be alone for ever.   We two—this crown—
I half remember.   It has been in my dreams.
Bend lower, O king, that I may crown you
        with it.
O flower of the branch, O bird among the
        leaves,
O silver fish that my two hands have taken
Out of the running stream, O morning star,
Trembling in the blue heavens like a white fawn
Upon the misty border of the wood,
Bend lower, that I may cover you with my hair,
For we will gaze upon this world no longer.

   [*The scene darkens, and the harp once more begins
      to burn as with a faint fire.* FORGAEL *is
      kneeling at* DECTORA's *feet.*

FORGAEL.

[*Gathering* DECTORA's *hair about him.*]

Beloved, having dragged the net about us,
And knitted mesh to mesh, we grow immortal;
And that old harp awakens of itself
To cry aloud to the grey birds, and dreams,
That have had dreams for father, live in us.

APPENDIX I

ACTING VERSION OF

THE SHADOWY WATERS

FORGAEL
AIBRIC
SAILORS
DECTORA

THE scene is the same as in the text except that the sail is
dull copper colour. The poop rises several feet above the
stage, and from the overhanging stern hangs a lanthorn with
a greenish light. The sea or sky is represented by a semi-
circular cloth of which nothing can be seen except a dark
abyss, for the stage is lighted by arc-lights so placed upon a
bridge over the proscenium as to throw a perpendicular light
upon the stage. The light is dim, and there are deep shadows
which waver as if with the passage of clouds over the moon.
The persons are dressed in blue and green, and move but
little. Some sailors are discovered crouching by the sail.
Forgael is asleep and Aibric standing by the tiller on the
raised poop.

First Sailor. It is long enough, and too long, For-
gael has been bringing us through the waste places
of the great sea.

Second Sailor. We did not meet with a ship to
make a prey of these eight weeks, or any shore or
island to plunder or to harry. It is a hard thing,
age to be coming on me, and I not to get the chance

of doing a robbery that would enable me to live quiet and honest to the end of my lifetime.

First Sailor. We are out since the new moon. What is worse again, it is the way we are in a ship, the barrels empty and my throat shrivelled with drought, and nothing to quench it but water only.

Forgael [*in his sleep*]. Yes; there, there; that hair that is the colour of burning.

First Sailor. Listen to him now, calling out in his sleep.

Forgael [*in his sleep*]. That pale forehead, that hair the colour of burning.

First Sailor. Some crazy dream he is in, and believe me it is no crazier than the thought he has waking. He is not the first that has had the wits drawn out from him through shadows and fantasies.

Second Sailor. That is what ails him. I have been thinking it this good while.

First Sailor. Do you remember that galley we sank at the time of the full moon?

Second Sailor. I do. We were becalmed the same night, and he sat up there playing that old harp of his until the moon had set.

First Sailor. I was sleeping up there by the bulwark, and when I woke in the sound of the harp a change came over my eyes, and I could see very strange things. The dead were floating upon the sea yet, and it seemed as if the life that went out of every one of them had turned to the shape of a man-headed bird—grey they were, and they rose up of a sudden and called out with voices like our own, and flew away singing to the west. Words like this they were singing: 'Happiness beyond measure, happiness where the sun dies.'

Second Sailor. I understand well what they are doing. My mother used to be talking of birds of the sort. They are sent by the lasting watchers to lead men away from this world and its women to some place of shining women that cast no shadow, having lived before the making of the earth. But I have no mind to go following him to that place.

First Sailor. Let us creep up to him and kill him in his sleep.

Second Sailor. I would have made an end of him long ago, but that I was in dread of his harp. It is said that when he plays upon it he has power over all the listeners, with or without the body, seen or unseen, and any man that listens grows to be as mad as himself.

First Sailor. What way can he play it, being in his sleep?

Second Sailor. But who would be our captain then to make out a course from the Bear and the Pole-star, and to bring us back home?

First Sailor. I have that thought out. We must have Aibric with us. He knows the constellations as well as Forgael. He is a good hand with the sword. Join with us; be our captain, Aibric. We are agreed to put an end to Forgael, before he wakes. There is no man but will be glad of it when it is done. Join with us, and you will have the captain's share and profit.

Aibric. Silence! for you have taken Forgael's pay.

First Sailor. Little pay we have had this twelve-month. We would never have turned against him if he had brought us, as he promised, into seas that would be thick with ships. That was the bargain. What is the use of knocking about and fighting as

we do unless we get the chance to drink more wine
and kiss more women than lasting peaceable men
through their long lifetime? You will be as good a
leader as ever he was himself, if you will but join us.

Aibric. And do you think that I will join myself
To men like you, and murder him who has been
My master from my earliest childhood up?
No! nor to a world of men like you
When Forgael's in the other scale. Come! come!
I'll answer to more purpose when you have drawn
That sword out of its scabbard.

First Sailor. You have awaked him. We had best
go, for we have missed this chance.

Forgael. Have the birds passed us? I could hear
 your voice.
But there were others.

Aibric.   I have seen nothing pass.

Forgael. You are certain of it? I never wake from
 sleep
But that I am afraid they may have passed;
For they're my only pilots. I have not seen them
For many days, and yet there must be many
Dying at every moment in the world.

Aibric. They have all but driven you crazy, and
 already
The sailors have been plotting for your death,
And all the birds have cried into your ears
Has lured you on to death.

Forgael.   No; but they promised—

Aibric. I know their promises. You have told
 me all.
They are to bring you to unheard-of passion,
To some strange love the world knows nothing of,
Some ever-living woman as you think,

One that can cast no shadow, being unearthly.
But that's all folly.   Turn the ship about,
Sail home again, be some fair woman's friend ;
Be satisfied to live like other men,
And drive impossible dreams away.   The world
Has beautiful women to please every man.

Forgael. But he that gets their love after the fashion
Loves in brief longing and deceiving hope
And bodily tenderness, and finds that even
The bed of love, that in the imagination
Had seemed to be the giver of all peace,
Is no more than a wine cup in the tasting,
And as soon finished.

Aibric.   All that ever loved
Have loved that way—there is no other way.

Forgael. Yet never have two lovers kissed but they
Believed there was some other near at hand,
And almost wept because they could not find it.

Aibric. When they have twenty years; in middle life
They take a kiss for what a kiss is worth,
And let the dream go by.

Forgael.   It's not a dream,
But the reality that makes our passion
As a lamp shadow—no—no lamp, the sun.
What the world's million lips are thirsting for,
Must be substantial somewhere.

Aibric.   I have heard the Druids
Mutter such things as they awake from trance.
It may be that the dead have lit upon it,
Or those that never lived ; no mortal can.

Forgael. I only of all living men shall find it.

Aibric. Then seek it in the habitable world,
Or leap into that sea and end a journey
That has no other end.

Forgael.   I cannot answer.
I can see nothing plain; all's mystery.
Yet, sometimes there's a torch inside my head
That makes all clear, but when the light is gone
I have but images, analogies,
The mystic bread, the sacramental wine,
The red rose where the two shafts of the cross,
Body and soul, waking and sleep, death, life,
Whatever meaning ancient allegorists
Have settled on, are mixed into one joy.
For what's the rose but that? miraculous cries,
Old stories about mystic marriages,
Impossible truths?   But when the torch is lit
All that is impossible is certain,
I plunge in the abyss.

[Sailors *come in.*]

First Sailor. Look there! There in the mist! A ship of spices.

Second Sailor. We would not have noticed her but for the sweet smell through the air. Ambergris and sandalwood, and all the herbs the witches bring from the sunrise.

First Sailor. No; but opoponax and cinnamon.

Forgael [*taking the tiller from* AIBRIC]. The ever-living have kept my bargain; they have paid you on the nail.

Aibric. Take up that rope to make her fast while we are plundering her.

First Sailor. There is a king on her deck, and a queen. Where there is one woman it is certain there will be others.

Aibric. Speak lower or they'll hear.

First Sailor. They cannot hear; they are too much

taken up with one another. Look! he has stooped down and kissed her on the lips.

Second Sailor. When she finds out we have as good men aboard she may not be too sorry in the end.

First Sailor. She will be as dangerous as a wild cat. These queens think more of the riches and the great name they get by marriage than of a ready hand and a strong body.

Second Sailor. There is nobody is natural but a robber. That is the reason the whole world goes tottering about upon its bandy legs.

Aibric. Run upon them now, and overpower the crew while yet asleep.

[Sailors *and* AIBRIC *go out. The clashing of swords and confused voices are heard from the other ship, which cannot be seen because of the sail.*

Forgael [*who has remained at the tiller*]. There!
    there! They come! Gull, gannet, or diver,
But with a man's head, or a fair woman's.
They hover over the masthead awhile
To wait their friends, but when their friends have
    come
They'll fly upon that secret way of theirs,
One—and one—a couple—five together.
And now they all wheel suddenly and fly
To the other side, and higher in the air,
They've gone up thither, friend's run up by friend;
They've gone to their beloved ones in the air,
In the waste of the high air, that they may wander
Among the windy meadows of the dawn.
But why are they still waiting? Why are they
Circling and circling over the masthead?
Ah! now they all look down—they'll speak of me

What the ever-living put into their minds,
And of that shadowless unearthly woman
At the world's end. I hear the message now.
But it's all mystery. There's one that cries,
'From love and hate.' Before the sentence ends
Another breaks upon it with a cry,
'From love and death and out of sleep and waking.'
And with the cry another cry is mixed,
'What can we do, being shadows?' All mystery,
And I am drunken with a dizzy light.
But why do they still hover overhead?
Why are you circling there? Why do you linger?
Why do you not run to your desire?
Now that you have happy winged bodies.
Being too busy in the air, and the high air,
They cannot hear my voice. But why that circling?

> [*The* Sailors *have returned.* DECTORA *is with them.*
> *She is dressed in pale green, with copper ornaments*
> *on her dress, and has a copper crown upon her head.*
> *Her hair is dull red.*

> *Forgael* [*turning and seeing her*]. Why are you stand-
> ing with your eyes upon me?
You are not the world's core. O no, no, no!
That cannot be the meaning of the birds.
You are not its core. My teeth are in the world,
But have not bitten yet.
> *Dectora.*   I am a queen,
And ask for satisfaction upon these
Who have slain my husband and laid hands upon me.
> *Forgael.* I'd set my hopes on one that had no
> shadow,—
Where do you come from? who brought you to this
place?
Why do you cast a shadow? Answer me that.

Dectora. Would that the storm that overthrew my
     ships,
And drowned the treasures of nine conquered nations,
And blew me hither to my lasting sorrow,
Had drowned me also.   But, being yet alive,
I ask a fitting punishment for all
That raised their hands against him.
     Forgael.   There are some
That weigh and measure all in these waste seas—
They that have all the wisdom that's in life,
And all that prophesying images
Made of dim gold rave out in secret tombs ;
They have it that the plans of kings and queens
Are dust on the moth's wing ; that nothing matters
But laughter and tears—laughter, laughter, and tears—
That every man should carry his own soul
Upon his shoulders.
     Dectora.   You've nothing but wild words,
And I would know if you would give me vengeance.
     Forgael. When she finds out that I'll not let her go—
When she knows that.
     Dectora.   What is it that you are muttering—
That you'll not let me go ?   I am a queen.
     Forgael. Although you are more beautiful than any,
I almost long that it were possible;
But if I were to put you on that ship,
With sailors that were sworn to do your will,
And you had spread a sail for home, a wind
Would rise of a sudden, or a wave so huge,
It had washed among the stars and put them out,
And beat the bulwark of your ship on mine,
Until you stood before me on the deck—
As now.
     Dectora. Does wandering in these desolate seas

And listening to the cry of wind and wave
Bring madness?

    Forgael.   Queen, I am not mad.

    Dectora. And yet you say the water and the wind
Would rise against me.

    Forgael.   No, I am not mad—
If it be not that hearing messages
From lasting watchers that outlive the moon
At the most quiet midnight is to be stricken.

    Dectora. And did those watchers bid you take me
        captive?

    Forgael. Both you and I are taken in the net.
It was their hands that plucked the winds awake
And blew you hither; and their mouths have
        promised
I shall have love in their immortal fashion.
They gave me that old harp of the nine spells
That is more mighty than the sun and moon,
Or than the shivering·casting-net of the stars,
That none might take you from me.

    Dectora [*first trembling back from the mast where the
harp is, and then laughing*]. For a moment
Your raving of a message and a harp
More mighty than the stars half troubled me.
But all that's raving. Who is there can compel
The daughter and grand-daughter of a king
To be his bedfellow?

    Forgael.   Until your lips
Have called me their beloved, I'll not kiss them.

    Dectora. My husband and my king died at my
        feet,
And yet you talk of love.

    Forgael.   The movement of time
Is shaken in these seas, and what one does

One moment has no might upon the moment
That follows after.
   Dectora.   I understand you now.
You have a Druid craft of wicked sound.
Wrung from the cold women of the sea—
A magic that can call a demon up,
Until my body give you kiss for kiss.
   Forgael. Your soul shall give the kiss.
   Dectora.   I am not afraid,
While there's a rope to run into a noose
Or wave to drown. But I have done with words,
And I would have you look into my face
And know that it is fearless.
   Forgael.   Do what you will,
For neither I nor you can break a mesh
Of the great golden net that is about us.
   Dectora. There's nothing in the world that's worth
     a fear.

   [*She passes* FORGAEL *and stands for a moment looking
     into his face.*]
I have good reason for that thought.
   [*She runs suddenly on to the raised part of the poop.*]
                        And now
I can put fear away as a queen should.
[*She mounts on the bulwark and turns towards* FORGAEL.]
Fool, fool! Although you have looked into my face
You did not see my purpose. I shall have gone
Before a hand can touch me.
   Forgael [*folding his arms*]. My hands are still;
The ever-living hold us. Do what you will,
You cannot leap out of the golden net.
   First Sailor. There is no need for you to drown.
                                 R

Give us our pardon and we will bring you home on
your own ship, and make an end of this man that is
leading us to death.

Dectora. I promise it.

Aibric.   I am on his side.
I'd strike a blow for him to give him time
To cast his dreams away.

First Sailor. He has put a sudden darkness over
the moon.

Dectora. Nine swords with handles of rhinoceros
    horn
To him that strikes him first.

First Sailor. I will strike him first. No! for that
music of his might put a beast's head upon my
shouders, or it may be two heads and they devour-
ing one another.

Dectora. I'll give a golden galley full of fruit
That has the heady flavour of new wine
To him that wounds him to the death.

First Sailor. I'll strike at him. His spells, when he
dies, will die with him and vanish away.

Second Sailor. I'll strike at him.

The Others. And I! And I! And I!

[FORGAEL *plays upon the harp.*]

First Sailor [*falling into a dream*]. It is what they
are saying, there is some person dead in the other
ship; we have to go and wake him. They did not say
what way he came to his end, but it was sudden.

Second Sailor. You are right, you are right. We
have to go to that wake.

Dectora. He has flung a Druid spell upon the air,
And set you dreaming.

Second Sailor. What way can we raise a keen, not
knowing what name to call him by?

First Sailor. Come on to his ship. His name will come to mind in a moment. All I know is he died a thousand years ago, and was never yet waked.

Second Sailor. How can we wake him having no ale?

First Sailor. I saw a skin of ale aboard her—a pigskin of brown ale.

Third Sailor. Come to the ale, a pigskin of brown ale, a goatskin of yellow.

First Sailor [*singing*]. Brown ale and yellow; yellow and brown ale; a goatskin of yellow.

All [*singing*]. Brown ale and yellow; yellow and brown ale!   [*Sailors go out.*

Dectora. Protect me now, gods, that my people swear by!

[AIBRIC *has risen from the ground where he had fallen. He has begun looking for his sword as if in a dream.*

Aibric. Where is my sword that fell out of my hand
When I first heard the news? Ah, there it is!

[*He goes dreamily towards the sword, but* DECTORA *runs at it and takes it up before he can reach it.*

Aibric [*sleepily*]. Queen, give it me.
Dectora.   No, I have need of it.
Aibric. Why do you need a sword? But you may keep it,
Now that he's dead I have no need of it,
For everything is gone.

A Sailor [*calling from the other ship*]. Come hither, Aibric,
And tell me who it is that we are waking.

Aibric [*half to* DECTORA, *half to himself*]. What name had that dead king? Arthur of Britain?
No, no—not Arthur. I remember now.

It was golden-armed Iollan, and he died
Brokenhearted, having lost his queen
Through wicked spells. That is not all the tale,
For he was killed. O ! O ! O ! O ! O ! O !
For golden-armed Iollan has been killed.

[*He goes out. While he has been speaking, and through
part of what follows, one hears the singing of the
SAILORS from the other ship. DECTORA stands with
the sword lifted in front of FORGAEL. He changes
the tune.*

Dectora. I will end all your magic on the instant.

[*Her voice becomes dreamy, and she lowers the sword
slowly, and finally lets it fall. She spreads out her
hair. She takes off her crown and lays it upon the
deck.*

The sword is to lie beside him in the grave.
It was in all his battles. I will spread my hair,
And wring my hands, and wail him bitterly,
For I have heard that he was proud and laughing,
Blue-eyed, and a quick runner on bare feet,
And that he died a thousand years ago.
O ! O ! O !

[FORGAEL *changes the tune.*]
But no, that is not it.
I knew him well, and while I heard him laughing
They killed him at my feet. O ! O ! O ! O !
For golden-armed Iollan that I loved.
But what is it that made me say I loved him?
It was that harper put it in my thoughts,
But it is true. Why did they run upon him,
And beat the golden helmet with their swords ?

Forgael. Do you not know me, lady ? I am he
That you are weeping for.

Dectora.   No, for he is dead.
O! O! O! for golden-armed Iollan.
  Forgael. It was so given out, but I will prove
That the grave-diggers in a dreamy frenzy
Have buried nothing but my golden arms.
Listen to that low-laughing string of the moon
And you will recollect my face and voice,
For you have listened to me playing it
These thousand years.

  [*He starts up, listening to the birds. The harp slips
  from his hands, and remains leaning against the bul-
  warks behind him.*

                      What are the birds at there?
Why are they all a-flutter of a sudden?
What are you calling out above the mast?
If railing and reproach and mockery
Because I have awakened her to love
By magic strings, I'll make this answer to it:
Being driven on by voices and by dreams
That were clear messages from the ever-living,
I have done right.   What could I but obey?
And yet you make a clamour of reproach.
  Dectora [*laughing*]. Why, it's a wonder out of
      reckoning
That I should keen him from the full of the moon
To the horn, and he be hale and hearty.
  Forgael. How have I wronged her now that she is
      merry?
But no, no, no! your cry is not against me.
You know the councils of the ever-living,
And all the tossing of your wings is joy,
And all that murmuring's but a marriage song;
But if it be reproach, I answer this:

There is not one among you that made love
By any other means.   You call it passion,
Consideration, generosity;
But it was all deceit, and flattery
To win a woman in her own despite,
For love is war, and there is hatred in it;
And if you say that she came willingly—
   Dectora. Why do you turn away and hide your face,
That I would look upon for ever?
    Forgael.   My grief.
    Dectora. Have I not loved you for a thousand
      years?
    Forgael. I never have been golden-armed Iollan.
    Dectora. I do not understand.   I know your face
Better than my own hands.
    Forgael.   I have deceived you
Out of all reckoning.
    Dectora.   Is it not true
That you were born a thousand years ago,
In islands where the children of Aengus wind
In happy dances under a windy moon,
And that you'll bring me there?
    Forgael.   I have deceived you;
I have deceived you utterly.
    Dectora.   How can that be?
Is it that though your eyes are full of love
Some other woman has a claim on you,
And I've but half?
    Forgael.   Oh, no!
    Dectora.   And if there is,
If there be half a hundred more, what matter?
I'll never give another thought to it;
No, no, nor half a thought; but do not speak.
Women are hard and proud and stubborn-hearted,

Their heads being turned with praise and flattery;
And that is why their lovers are afraid
To tell them a plain story.

Forgael.   That's not the story;
But I have done so great a wrong against you,
There is no measure that it would not burst.
I will confess it all.

Dectora.   What do I care,
Now that my body has begun to dream,
And you have grown to be a burning coal
In the imagination and intellect?
If something that's most fabulous were true—
If you had taken me by magic spells,
And killed a lover or husband at my feet—
I would not let you speak, for I would know
That it was yesterday and not to-day
I loved him; I would cover up my ears,
As I am doing now. [*A pause.*] Why do you weep?

Forgael. I weep because I've nothing for your eyes
But desolate waters and a battered ship.

Dectora. O, why do you not lift your eyes to mine?

Forgael. I weep—I weep because bare night's above,
And not a roof of ivory and gold.

Dectora. I would grow jealous of the ivory roof,
And strike the golden pillars with my hands.
I would that there was nothing in the world
But my beloved—that night and day had perished,
And all that is and all that is to be,
All that is not the meeting of our lips.

Forgael. Why do you turn your eyes upon bare
      night?
Am I to fear the waves, or is the moon
My enemy?

Dectora. I looked upon the moon,

Longing to knead and pull it into shape
That I might lay it on your head as a crown.
But now it is your thoughts that wander away,
For you are looking at the sea. Do you not know
How great a wrong it is to let one's thought
Wander a moment when one is in love?

[*He has moved away. She follows him. He is looking
out over the sea, shading his eyes.*

Dectora. Why are you looking at the sea?
Forgael.   Look there!
There where the cloud creeps up upon the moon.
Dectora. What is there but a troop of ash-grey birds
That fly into the west?

[*The scene darkens, but there is a ray of light upon the
figures.*

Forgael.   But listen, listen!
Dectora. What is there but the crying of the birds?
Forgael. If you'll but listen closely to that crying
You'll hear them calling out to one another
With human voices.
Dectora.   Clouds have hid the moon.
The birds cry out, what can I do but tremble?
Forgael. They have been circling over our heads
     in the air,
But now that they have taken to the road
We have to follow, for they are our pilots;
They're crying out. Can you not hear their cry—
'There is a country at the end of the world
Where no child's born but to outlive the moon.'

[*The* Sailors *come in with* AIBRIC. *They carry torches.*]

Aibric. We have lit upon a treasure that's so great
Imagination cannot reckon it.

The hold is full—boxes of precious spice,
Ivory images with amethyst eyes,
Dragons with eyes of ruby.   The whole ship
Flashes as if it were a net of herrings.
Let us return to our own country, Forgael,
And spend it there. Have you not found this queen?
What more have you to look for on the seas?
   Forgael. I cannot—I am going on to the end.
As for this woman, I think she is coming with me.
   Aibric. Speak to him, lady, and bid him turn the
    ship.
He knows that he is taking you to death;
He cannot contradict me.
   Dectora.   Is that true?
   Forgael. I do not know for certain.
   Dectora.   Carry me
To some sure country, some familiar place.
Have we not everything that life can give
In having one another?
   Forgael.   How could I rest
If I refused the messengers and pilots
With all those sights and all that crying out?
   Dectora. I am a woman, I die at every breath.
   Aibric [*to the* Sailors]. To the other ship, for there's
    no help in words,
And I will follow you and cut the rope
When I have said farewell to this man here,
For neither I nor any living man
Will look upon his face again.

   [Sailors *go out, leaving one torch perhaps in a torch-*
    holder on the bulwark.

   Forgael [*to* DECTORA].   Go with him,
For he will shelter you and bring you home.
   Aibric [*taking* FORGAEL's *hand*]. I'll do it for his sake.

Dectora.   No.   Take this sword
And cut the rope, for I go on with Forgael.
  Aibric. Farewell! Farewell!
                    [*He goes out.   The light grows stronger.*
  Dectora.   The sword is in the rope—
The rope's in two—it falls into the sea,
It whirls into the foam.   O ancient worm,
Dragon that loved the world and held us to it,
You are broken, you are broken.   The world drifts
      away,
And I am left alone with my beloved,
Who cannot put me from his sight for ever.
We are alone for ever, and I laugh,
Forgael, because you cannot put me from you.
The mist has covered the heavens, and you and I
Shall be alone for ever.   We two—this crown—
I half remember.   It has been in my dreams.
Bend lower, O king, that I may crown you with it.
O flower of the branch, O bird among the leaves,
O silver fish that my two hands have taken
Out of the running stream, O morning star,
Trembling in the blue heavens like a white fawn
Upon the misty border of the wood,
Bend lower, that I may cover you with my hair,
For we will gaze upon this world no longer.

      [*The harp begins to burn as with fire.*]

  Forgael [*gathering* DECTORA's *hair about him*].

        Beloved, having dragged the net about us,
And knitted mesh to mesh, we grow immortal;
And that old harp awakens of itself
To cry aloud to the grey birds, and dreams,
That have had dreams for father, live in us.

APPENDIX II.

A DIFFERENT VERSION OF DEIRDRE'S ENTRANCE.

After the first performance of this play in the autumn of
1906, I rewrote the play up to the opening of the scene
where Naisi and Deirdre play chess. The new version was
played in the spring of 1907, and after that I rewrote from
the entrance of Deirdre to her questioning the musicians,
but felt, though despairing of setting it right, that it was
still mere bones, mere dramatic logic. The principal diffi-
culty with the form of dramatic structure I have adopted is
that, unlike the loose Elizabethan form, it continually forces
one by its rigour of logic away from one's capacities, ex-
periences, and desires, until, if one have not patience to
wait for the mood, or to rewrite again and again till it comes,
there is rhetoric and logic and dry circumstance where
there should be life. After the version printed in the text
of this book had gone to press, Mrs. Patrick Campbell came
to our Abbey Theatre and, liking what she saw there, offered
to come and play Deirdre among us next November, and
this so stirred my imagination that the scene came right in
a moment. It needs some changes in the stage directions at
the beginning of the play. There is no longer need for loaf
and flagon, but the women at the braziers should when the
curtain rises be arraying themselves—the one holding a
mirror for the other perhaps. The play then goes on un-
changed till the entrance of Deirdre, when the following
scene is substituted for that on pages 139-140. (Bodb is
pronounced Bove.)

DEIRDRE, NAISI *and* FERGUS *enter*. DEIRDRE *is carrying a little embroidered*
bag. She goes over towards the women.

DEIRDRE.

Silence your music, though I thank you for it;
But the wind's blown upon my hair, and I
Must set the jewels on my neck and head
For one that's coming.

NAISI.

Your colour has all gone
As 'twere with fear, and there's no cause for that.

DEIRDRE.

These women have the raddle that they use
To make them brave and confident, although
Dread, toil or cold may chill the blood o' their cheeks.
You'll help me, women.   It is my husband's will
I show my trust in one that may be here
Before the mind can call the colour up.
My husband took these rubies from a king
Of Surracha that was so murderous
He seemed all glittering dragon.   Now wearing them
Myself wars on myself, for I myself—
That do my husband's will, yet fear to do it—
Grow dragonish to myself.

[*The* Women *have gathered about her.* NAISI *has stood looking at her,*
but FERGUS *leads him to the chess-table.*

FERGUS.

We'll play at chess
Till the king come.   It is but natural
That she should fear him, for her house has been
The hole of the badger and the den of the fox.

NAISI.

If I were childish and had faith in omens
I'd rather not have lit on that old chessboard
At my homecoming.

FERGUS.

There's a tale about it,—
It has been lying there these many years,—
Some wild old sorrowful tale.

NAISI.

It is the board
Where Lugaidh Redstripe and that wife of his
Who had a seamew's body half the year
Played at the chess upon the night they died.

FERGUS.

I can remember now: a tale of treachery,
A broken promise and a journey's end.
But it were best forgot.

[DEIRDRE *has been standing with the women about her. They have been*
helping her to put on her jewels and to put the pigment on her cheeks and
arrange her hair.   She has gradually grown attentive to what FERGUS
is saying.

NAISI.

If the tale's true,—
When it was plain that they had been betrayed,
They moved the men and waited for the end
As it were bedtime, and had so quiet minds
They hardly winked their eyes when the sword flashed.

FERGUS.

She never could have played so, being a woman,
If she had not the cold sea's blood in her.

DEIRDRE.

I have heard the ever-living warn mankind
By changing clouds and casual accidents
Or what seem so.

NAISI.

Stood th' ever-living there,
Old Lir and Aengus from his glassy tower,
And that hill-haunting Bodb to warn us hence,—
Our honour is so knitted up with staying,
King Conchubar's word and Fergus' word being pledged,
I'd brave them out and stay.

DEIRDRE.

No welcomer,
And a bare house upon the journey's end!
Is that the way a king that means no wrong
Honours a guest?

FERGUS.

He is but making ready
A welcome in his house, arranging where
The moorhen and the mallard go, and where
The speckled heath-cock in a golden dish.

DEIRDRE.

Has he no messenger—

[Etc., etc.]

The play then goes on unchanged, except that on page
151, instead of the short speech of Deirdre, beginning
'Safety and peace,' one should read

'Safety and peace!
I had them when a child, but from that hour
I have found life obscure and violent,
And think that I shall find it so for ever.'

APPENDIX III.

The Legendary and Mythological Foundation of the Plays.

The greater number of the stories I have used, and persons I have spoken of, are in Lady Gregory's *Gods and Fighting Men* and *Cuchulain of Muirthemne*. If my small Dublin audience for poetical drama grows to any size, whether now or at some future time, I shall owe it to these two books, masterpieces of prose, which can but make the old stories as familiar to Irishmen at anyrate as are the stories of Arthur and his Knights to all readers of books. I cannot believe that it is from friendship that I weigh these books with Malory, and feel no discontent at the tally, or that it is the wish to make the substantial origin of my own art familiar, that would make me give them before all other books to young men and girls in Ireland. I wrote for the most part before they were written, but all, or all but all, is there. I took the Aengus and Edain of *The Shadowy Waters* from poor translations of the various Aengus stories, which, new translated by Lady Gregory, make up so much of what is most beautiful in both her books. They had, however, so completely become a part of my own thought that in 1897, when I was still working on an early version of *The Shadowy Waters*, I saw one night with my bodily eyes, as it seemed, two beautiful persons, who would, I believe, have answered to their names. The plot of the play itself has, however, no definite old story for its foundation, but was woven to a very great extent out of certain visionary experiences.

The foundations of *Deirdre* and of *On Baile's Strand* are stories called respectively the 'Fate of the Sons of Usnach' and 'The Son of Aoife' in *Cuchulain of Muirthemne*.

The King's Threshold is, however, founded upon a middle-Irish story of the demands of the poets at the Court of King Guaire of Gort, but I have twisted it about and revised its moral that the poet might have the best of it. It owes something to a play on the same subject by my old friend Edwin Ellis, who heard the story from me and wrote of it long ago.

APPENDIX IV.

The King's Threshold was first played October 7th, 1903, in the Molesworth Hall, Dublin, by the Irish National Theatre Society, and with the following cast:

Seanchan	Frank Fay
King Guaire	P. Kelly
Lord High Chamberlain	Seumus O'Sullivan
Soldier	William Conroy
Monk	S. Sheridan-Neill
Mayor	William Fay
A Cripple	Patrick Colum
A Court Lady	Honor Lavelle
Another Court Lady	Dora Melville
A Princess	Sara Algood
Another Princess	Dora Gunning
Fedelm	Maire ni Shiubhlaigh
A Servant	P. MacShiubhlaigh
Another Servant	P. Josephs
A Pupil	G. Roberts
Another Pupil	Cartia MacCormac

It has been revised a good many times since then, and although the play has not been changed in the radical structure, the parts of the Mayor, Servant, and Cripple are altogether new, and the rest is altered here and there. It was written when our Society was beginning its fight for the recognition of pure art in a community of which one half is buried in the practical affairs of life, and the other half in politics and a propagandist patriotism.

On Baile's Strand was first played, in a version considerably different from the present, on December 27th, 1904, at the opening of the Abbey Theatre, Dublin, and with the following cast:

Cuchulain . . . . . Frank Fay
Conchubar . . . . George Roberts
Daire *(an old King not now in the play)* G. MacDonald
The Blind Man . . Seumus O'Sullivan
The Fool . . . . William Fay
The Young Man . . P. MacShiubhlaigh

The old and young kings were played by the following:
R. Nash, A. Power, U. Wright, E. Keegan, Emma Vernon,
Dora Gunning, Sara Algood. It was necessary to put women
into men's parts owing to the smallness of our company at
that time.

The play was revived by the National Theatre Society,
Ltd., in a somewhat altered version at Oxford, Cambridge,
and London a few months later. I then entirely rewrote it
up to the entrance of the Young Man, and changed it a
good deal from that on to the end, and this new version
was played at the Abbey Theatre for the first time in
April, 1906.

The first version of *The Shadowy Waters* was first per-
formed on January 14th, 1904, in the Molesworth Hall,
Dublin, with the following players in the principal parts:

Forgael . . . . . Frank Fay
Aibric . . . . Seumus O'Sullivan
Dectora . . . Maire ni Shiubhlaigh

Its production was an accident, for in the first instance I
had given it to the company that they might have some
practice in the speaking of my sort of blank verse until I
had a better play finished. It played badly enough from the
point of view of any ordinary playgoer, but pleased many of
my friends; and as I had been in America when it was
played, I got it played again privately, and gave it to Miss
Farr for a Theosophical Convention, that I might discover
how to make a better play of it. I then completely rewrote
it in the form that it has in the text of this book, but this

S

version had once again to be condensed and altered for its production in Dublin, 1906. Mr. Sinclair took the part of Aibric, and Miss Darragh that of Dectora, while Mr. Frank Fay was Forgael as before. It owed a considerable portion of what success it met with both in its new and old form to a successful colour scheme and to dreamy movements and intonations on the part of the players. The scenery for its performance in 1906 was designed by Mr. Robert Gregory.

Deirdre was first played at the Abbey Theatre, Dublin, on November 27th, 1906, with Miss Darragh as Deirdre, Mr. Frank Fay as Naisi, Mr. Sinclair as Fergus, Mr. Kerrigan as Conchubar, and Miss Sara Algood, Miss McNeill, and Miss O'Dempsey as the Musicians. The scenery was by Mr. Robert Gregory.

Printed by A. H. BULLEN, *at The Shakespeare Head Press,*
Stratford-on-Avon.

Trieste Publishing has a massive catalogue of classic book titles. Our aim is to provide readers with the highest quality reproductions of fiction and non-fiction literature that has stood the test of time. The many thousands of books in our collection have been sourced from libraries and private collections around the world.

The titles that Trieste Publishing has chosen to be part of the collection have been scanned to simulate the original. Our readers see the books the same way that their first readers did decades or a hundred or more years ago. Books from that period are often spoiled by imperfections that did not exist in the original. Imperfections could be in the form of blurred text, photographs, or missing pages. It is highly unlikely that this would occur with one of our books. Our extensive quality control ensures that the readers of Trieste Publishing's books will be delighted with their purchase. Our staff has thoroughly reviewed every page of all the books in the collection, repairing, or if necessary, rejecting titles that are not of the highest quality. This process ensures that the reader of one of Trieste Publishing's titles receives a volume that faithfully reproduces the original, and to the maximum degree possible, gives them the experience of owning the original work.

We pride ourselves on not only creating a pathway to an extensive reservoir of books of the finest quality, but also providing value to every one of our readers. Generally, Trieste books are purchased singly - on demand, however they may also be purchased in bulk. Readers interested in bulk purchases are invited to contact us directly to enquire about our tailored bulk rates. Email: customerservice@triestepublishing.com

You May Also Like

ISBN: 9780649565733
Paperback: 170 pages
Dimensions: 6.14 x 0.36 x 9.21 inches
Language: eng

Longmans' English Classics; Dryden's Palamon and Arcite

William Tenney Brewster

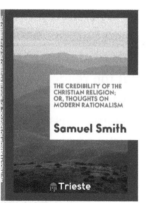

ISBN: 9780649557516
Paperback: 204 pages
Dimensions: 5.83 x 0.43 x 8.27 inches
Language: eng

The Credibility of the Christian Religion; Or, Thoughts on Modern Rationalism

Samuel Smith

www.triestepublishing.com

You May Also Like

ISBN: 9780649066155
Paperback: 144 pages
Dimensions: 6.14 x 0.31 x 9.21 inches
Language: eng

Heath's Modern Language Series. Atala

François-René de Chateaubriand & Oscar Kuhns

ISBN: 9780649731213
Paperback: 160 pages
Dimensions: 6.14 x 0.34 x 9.21 inches
Language: eng

War Poems, 1898

California Club & Irving M. Scott

You May Also Like

Report of the Department of Farms and Markets, pp. 5-71

Various

ISBN: 9780649333158
Paperback: 84 pages
Dimensions: 6.14 x 0.17 x 9.21 inches
Language: eng

Catalogue of the Episcopal Theological School in Cambridge Massachusetts, 1891-1892

Various

ISBN: 9780649324132
Paperback: 78 pages
Dimensions: 6.14 x 0.16 x 9.21 inches
Language: eng

You May Also Like

ISBN: 9780649352142
Paperback: 88 pages
Dimensions: 6.14 x 0.18 x 9.21 inches
Language: eng

Three Hundred Tested Recipes

Various

ISBN: 9780649419418
Paperback: 108 pages
Dimensions: 6.14 x 0.22 x 9.21 inches
Language: eng

A Basket of Fragments

Anonymous

Find more of our titles on our website. We have a selection of thousands of titles that will interest you. Please visit

www.triestepublishing.com

Lightning Source UK Ltd.
Milton Keynes UK
UKHW02f1008010618
323578UK00004B/342/P